CAMBRIDGE
UNIVERSITY PRESS

CAMBRIDGE
Primary English

Workbook 6

Sally Burt & Debbie Ridgard

CAMBRIDGE
UNIVERSITY PRESS

University Printing House, Cambridge CB2 8BS, United Kingdom

One Liberty Plaza, 20th Floor, New York, NY 10006, USA

477 Williamstown Road, Port Melbourne, VIC 3207, Australia

314–321, 3rd Floor, Plot 3, Splendor Forum, Jasola District Centre,
New Delhi – 110025, India

103 Penang Road, #05–06/07, Visioncrest Commercial Singapore 238467

Cambridge University Press is part of the University of Cambridge.

It furthers the University's mission by disseminating knowledge in the pursuit of
education, learning and research at the highest international levels of excellence.

www.cambridge.org Information on this title: www.cambridge.org/9781108746281

First published 2015
Second edition 2021

20 19 18 17 16 15 14 13 12 11 10 9 8 7 6 5

Printed in Italy by Rotolito S.p.A.

A catalogue record for this publication is available from the British Library.

ISBN 978-1-108-74628-1 Paperback with Digital Access (1 Year)

Cambridge University Press has no responsibility for the persistence or accuracy
of URLs for external or third-party internet websites referred to in this publication,
and does not guarantee that any content on such websites is, or will remain, accurate
or appropriate. Information regarding prices, travel timetables, and other factual
information given in this work is correct at the time of first printing but Cambridge
University Press does not guarantee the accuracy of such information thereafter.

....

Contents

› Acknowledgements

The authors and publishers acknowledge the following sources of copyright material and are grateful for the permissions granted. While every effort has been made, it has not always been possible to identify the sources of all the material used, or to trace all copyright holders. If any omissions are brought to our notice, we will be happy to include the appropriate acknowledgements on reprinting.

Unit 6 Poem 'One Day' by Tyrone August, 1982. Reproduced with the permission of the author Dr Tyrone August, Journalist and writer based in Cape Town, South Africa; **Unit 7** Text © 2013 Kate DiCamillo Illustrations © 2013 Keith Campbell From *Flora & Ulysses* written by Kate DiCamillo and illustrated by K. G. Campbell Reproduced by permission of Walker Books Ltd, London SE11 5HJ www.walker.co.uk; **Unit 9** 'How to Cut a Pomegranate' from *The Terrorist at My Table* by Imtiaz Dharker (Bloodaxe Books, 2006). Reproduced with permission of Bloodaxe Books. www.bloodaxebooks.com;

Thanks to the following for permission to reproduce images:

Cover image by Omar Aranda (Beehive Illustration); *Inside;* **Unit 1** Mint Images/GI; Sharply-Done/GI; **Unit 2** Viktar/GI; Prakash Mathema/AFP/GI; Universal History Archive/GI; David Oliver/GI; Lightfieldstudios/GI; **Unit 3** Mandy Disher Photography/GI; Peter Cade/GI; Indeed/GI; **Unit 4** Juana Mari Moya/GI; Andrzej Wojcicki/GI; Gremlin/GI; **Unit 5** Oscar Tarneberg/GI; Alexander Friedrich/500px/GI; Karsten Wrobel/GI; Filo/GI; **Unit 6** Sean Gladwell/GI; Andrew_Howe/GI; **Unit 7** Stuart Shore, Wight Wildlfie Photography/GI; Funky-Data/GI; **Unit 8** Jenny Vaughan/AFP/GI; Andreusk/GI; Ondacaracola Photography/GI; Olga Nikiforova/GI; Ariel Skelley/GI; Peter Dazeley/GI; **Unit 9** Gresei/GI; Sabrina Bekeschus/GI; Gustavo Castillo/GI; Johner Images/GI

Key: GI= Getty Images

How to use this book

Workbook 6 provides questions for you to practise what you have learnt in class. There is a unit to match each unit in Learner's Book 6. Within each unit there are six or twelve sessions. Each session is divided into three parts:

Focus: These questions help you to master the basics. ⟶

> **Focus**
>
> 1 Say who or what the <u>underlined</u> pronouns refer to.
>
>   a The children love the apples you bought from the seller. <u>They</u> are delicious.
>
>   _____
>
>   b The interviewer asked the children questions. <u>He</u> wasn't sure who answered <u>them</u> first.
>
>   _____
>
>   c The guides saw the climbers leave the camp. Some went missing but <u>they</u> found <u>them</u>.
>
>   _____

Practice: These questions help ⟶ you to become more confident in using what you have learnt.

> **Practice**
>
> 2 Rewrite each sentence, adding the additional information in brackets using one or two dashes.
>
>   **Examples:** My brother took me to school. (the older one)
>
>   My brother – the older one – took me to school.
>
>   a The box was full of interesting things. (things I had never seen before)
>
>   _____

Challenge: These questions will ⟶ make you think more deeply.

> **Challenge**
>
> 3 Write whether the dash signals a dramatic pause leading to a climax or anti-climax, an aside or comment, or additional information.
>
>   a Elise ran crazily down the road – then screamed for help.
>
>   _____
>
>   b When I went to the cinema – the Cinema Max on Main Road – I saw my cousin.
>
>   _____

1 ▸ Different voices – different times

› 1.1 What is a prologue?

> The word prologue comes from an ancient Greek word, πρόλογος *(prológos)*, which is made from the prefix *pro* ('before') and the root word *lógos* ('word').

Focus

> **Pro** has more than one meaning when used as a prefix:
> 1 for (a substitute);
> 2 for (in favour of);
> 3 going or putting forward;
> 4 coming before.

1   Use the context of each sentence to decide on the meaning of the prefix in the words in **bold**. Write the corresponding number next to each sentence.

   a   The school is **promoting** healthy eating this week.   ——

   b   We debated the **pros** and cons of uniform in last week's assembly.   ——

   c   The doctor carried out a life-saving **procedure** on the baby.   ——

   d   As soon as I had read the **prologue**, I knew I would enjoy this book.   ——

   e   **Pronouns** stand in for nouns to prevent repetition.   ——

2 Choose three words from the boxes and write a sentence for each
   to demonstrate that you understand their meanings.

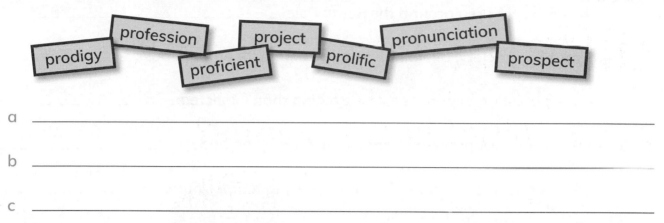

a _____

b _____

c _____

Practice

3 **Anti** (also **ant**) meaning 'against' or 'opposite' can be an antonym for **pro**.
   Choose the correct words from the boxes to match each definition on the next page.
   Only use a dictionary to check your answers at the end.

Don't confuse **anti** with **ante** – **ante** means *before*: <u>ante</u>chamber, <u>ante</u>cedent.

a   A substance produced in your blood to fight disease: _____

b   The very cold area around the South Pole: _____

c   Harmful to society; avoiding spending time with other people: _____

d   A disappointing experience, less exciting than expected: _____

e   A medicine that prevents harmful bacteria in the body: _____

f   A liquid added to water to lower its freezing temperature: _____

g   The exact opposite; a contrast between two things: _____

h   A chemical used to prevent infection in an injury: _____

i   A chemical to limit the effects of poison: _____

j   In the opposite direction to the movement of the hands of a clock: _____

Challenge

4   Choose the correct prefixes from the boxes to complete each word. Then use a dictionary to write the meaning of the prefix next to each completed word.

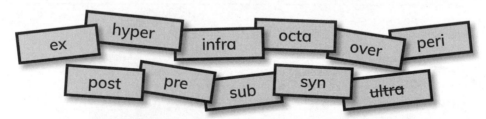

Example: <u>ultra</u> violet <u>extremely</u>

a   _____ cast   _____

b   _____ structure   _____

c _____ meter _____

d _____ pone _____

e _____ gon _____

f _____ active _____

g _____ pare _____

h _____ clude _____

i _____ merge _____

j _____ chronise _____

> 1.2 Delve into detail

Focus

1   Use the etymological dictionary entry to answer the questions.

> **Etymological dictionary entry**
>
> **phobia n**. An irrational or extreme fear of something. First recorded use in English c. 1786 possibly via French phobie. Originally the word was extracted from compound words using **phobia** as a suffix in ancient Greek, stemming from the Greek word φόβος (phobos) meaning fear, panic or terror.

> Many of the **suffixes** and **prefixes** we use originally came from ancient Greek or Latin words. Knowing the root word means you help unlock the meanings of other words containing the root word. Root words can appear as suffixes, prefixes or in the middle of words. Etymological dictionaries give the word's origin as well as its meaning.

a   What does 'phobia' mean? _____

b   What word class is it? _____

c   When was it first used in English? _____

d   What is the origin of the word? _____

_____

e   Use the word *phobia* in a sentence of your own.

_____

Practice

2   Circle all the words in the word search containing *phobia*.
Use a dictionary to help you.

> Search for *phobia* and then find the rest of the word. There are 12 words containing *phobia* in all. What does each one mean?

C	L	A	U	S	T	R	O	P	H	O	B	I	A	U
Z	E	K	I	T	G	F	E	G	J	B	V	J	I	X
K	M	R	A	B	D	H	H	R	A	G	S	T	B	C
T	Y	I	B	I	O	J	M	A	X	M	J	H	O	A
M	U	D	U	M	B	H	M	P	O	L	F	Q	H	R
I	B	I	B	L	I	O	P	H	O	B	I	A	P	N
A	B	L	U	T	O	P	H	O	B	I	A	U	O	O
K	K	X	G	O	U	R	Q	P	M	O	F	A	B	P
L	T	D	F	V	D	V	Z	H	O	H	G	S	R	H
O	A	I	B	O	H	P	O	O	Z	R	T	T	E	O
F	R	I	G	O	P	H	O	B	I	A	E	I	V	B
A	P	I	O	P	H	O	B	I	A	K	H	D	R	I
F	X	W	K	N	J	S	N	A	J	K	W	L	I	A
A	I	B	O	H	P	O	T	C	O	O	U	W	F	S
Q	C	V	S	X	F	Z	E	B	F	U	O	R	L	B

Challenge

3 Research three phobias from the word search using an etymological dictionary, if possible. Find out the meaning of each and write its origin. Follow the example.

Example: <u>auto</u> phobia <u>fear of being alone</u>
Etymology: <u>Greek autos (self)</u>

a _____ phobia _____ .

Etymology: _____ .

b _____ phobia _____ .

Etymology: _____ .

c _____ phobia _____ .

Etymology: _____ .

4 **Phil** is a word root meaning 'love' in ancient Greek. Choose the correct word from the boxes to complete these sentences and <u>underline</u> the root in each.

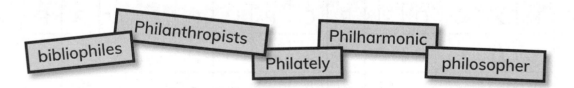

a Aristotle is a famous Ancient Greek _____ and scientist.

b _____ is the collection and study of postage stamps.

c _____ make charitable donations to promote human well-being.

d Many librarians are also _____ .

e The Vienna _____ Orchestra is a world-famous orchestra.

> 1.3 Focus on technique

Language focus

A **hyphen** is a short line that links words together to create one idea –
called a **compound word**.

Examples: eleven-year-old, sugar-free, twenty-nine, two-thirds, runner-up
Dashes are longer than hyphens. A single dash can signal:

- a dramatic pause leading to a climax or anti-climax

- an aside or comment

- additional information or contrast.

Example: She paused – then shouted 'Hooray!'

Focus

1 Choose whether to add a hyphen or a dash in the square brackets.

   a The passage was written in first [   ] person narrative.

   b There were twenty [ ] three runes on the box.

   c I opened the box and heard a sound [ ] an eerie sound like flute music.

   d My dad bought me an ice [ ] cream cake for my birthday.

   e I had so many presents [ ] more than I had ever hoped for.

Practice

2 Rewrite each sentence, adding the additional information in brackets
   using one or two dashes.

   Examples: My brother took me to school. (the older one)

   My brother – the older one – took me to school.

   a The box was full of interesting things. (things I had never seen before)

   _____

   b My school is the largest in the area. (the one on the corner)

   _____

c   Gardening is a relaxing weekend activity.
    (my favourite hobby)

_____

d   We managed to build the model aeroplane before everyone else. (working together)

_____

e   I wish my friend would tell me some of the folktales from her region.
    (the one from Kuala Lumpur)

_____

Challenge

3   Write whether the dash signals a dramatic pause leading to a climax or anti-climax,
    an aside or comment, or additional information.

a   Elise ran crazily down the road – then screamed for help.

_____

b   When I went to the cinema – the Cinema Max on Main Road – I saw my cousin.

_____

c   While I was playing sport – which as you know is my favourite thing – the
    principal came to watch.

_____

d   'What are we going to do – about the smashed window?' Lenny asked nervously.

_____

e   Runes – markings from ancient northern European alphabets – are often found
    by archaeologists.

_____

❭ 1.4 Write a short prologue

Prologuc

Long before we arrived, long before any of us arrived, a different people lived here. I feel Them here with me, watching, waiting, wary as the wind rustles through the trees and the river chatters over the lumpy pebbles.

We live close to a crossing; a shallow point in the river. It's not a road exactly but you can tell somehow that it was once a well-trodden path – the easiest way across the river. We use the bridge now, where the cars and trucks crash by, never noticing *the old way*. But I spend my time here, in the woods, sitting on the bank or following *the way* deep into the hills.

Sometimes I find things, things that tell me about Them. Sometimes I wonder if They leave them for me to find. A tiny carving of an animal – hard to tell what sort now – but tiny and perfectly carved from bone, I think. A pile of stones in a ring fused by time and weather into the ground. Holes gouged out of rock in a pattern, as if for a game of sorts. A painting on the rocks, faded but there.

Sometimes I know They are watching me, waiting for me to come and They walk with me as I venture further and further from where I know. One day, perhaps I will go too far but I trust They will always lead me home …

Focus

Make predictions from a prologue.

1   Read the prologue and answer the questions.

   a   What tense is the prologue mostly written in? _____

   b   Suggest a reason why this tense has been used.

   _____

   c   Why is the first sentence in a different tense?

   _____

   _____

d   Scan the prologue to find another example of a different tense. Why is it used?

_____

_____

Practice

2   Scan the prologue to answer these questions.

a   Is the prologue in first- or third-person narrative?

_____

b   Explain how you know. _____

c   Suggest why the author has written some words in italics.

_____

_____

d   What is the effect of certain personal pronouns being given a capital letter?

_____

_____

e   What is the purpose of the ellipsis (...) at the end of the prologue?

_____

f   Who do you think *They* are? _____

3   What genre of book do you predict this is going to be? Why?

_____

_____

_____

_____

Challenge

4   Make some predictions about the storyline.
     Use the questions in the box to help you.

Things to think about

- What sort of person is the main character?
- Why might the narrator spend so much time alone?
- Who could They be?
- Are the things the narrator finds clues? To what?
- What does the last line **foreshadow** about the plot?

Glossary

foreshadow suggest what is to come

_____

_____

_____

_____

_____

_____

_____

_____

> 1.5 White bears

Focus

Some words sound the same but are spelled differently like *bear* and *bare*.
They are called 'homophones'.

1   Match each homophone to its correct meaning.

a   [knead]   hit someone with your knee

[need]   press and shape the mixture firmly and repeatedly
with your hands to make bread

[kneed]   something you must have or do

b   [vain]   flat, narrow part of a fan, propeller, etc. that turns
because of the pressure of air or liquid against it

[vane]   tube that carries blood to the heart from the other
parts of the body

[vein]   too interested in your own appearance or achievements

Practice

2   Write sentences to show you know how to use each of the words in Activity 1.

a   _____

_____

_____

b   _____

_____

_____

Challenge

Some words are spelled the same but have multiple meanings.

3 Complete the word map showing the various meanings of the word *light*.

a

Word class: _____

Of comparatively little physical weight or density.

Antonym: _____

Example:

e

Word class: _____

Pale; having only a small amount of colouring.

Antonym: _____

Example:

b

Word class: _____

A flame from a match, etc. used to make a fire start burning.

Antonym: _____none_____

Example:

f

Word class: _____

The brightness that shines from the sun, from fire, or from electrical equipment, allowing you to see things.

Antonym: _____

Example: The light from the sun is dazzling.

Light

c

Word class: _____

Free from sadness or troubles.

Antonym: _____

Example:

g

Word class: _____

A device, usually electronic, which produces light.

Antonym: _____none_____

Example:

d

Word class: _____

Nimble, agile or sprightly, e.g. of foot or touch.

Antonym: _____

Example:

h

Word class: _____

To ignite or illuminate something.

Antonym: _____

Example:

4   Replace each example of *bright* with an appropriate synonym.

   a   The [*bright*] _____ light from that torch is very reassuring in this tunnel.

   b   That learner is so [*bright*] _____ that the school has offered her a scholarship.

   c   You seem to be in a [*bright*] _____ and breezy mood today.

> 1.6 Short and long sentences

Focus

1   Word order is important. Rewrite these sentences with correct punctuation and word order.

   a   White sense excellent an bears of smell have.

   b   anyone interviewed a white bear more who had ever seen to find out I.

   c   The white bear believe before hunting one everything you should know about the Sami.

2   Which sentences have more than one verb? _____

Practice

3   Extend each of these simple sentences by adding descriptive phrases.

   Example: __On his way to the forest__   Neddy ran __past the reindeer,__ __as fast as possible__.

   a   _____ the white bear stood up _____

   _____.

   b   _____ the deer scampered _____

   _____.

   c   _____ the peddler explained _____

   _____.

4   Underline the subject and verb in each of your sentences in Activity 3.

Challenge

5   Write your own sentences with one subject and one verb, extended by at least two phrases. The phrases can come before or after the subject and verb.

a   _____

_____

b   _____

_____

c   _____

_____

＞ 1.7 Review word classes

Language focus

Articles are the small words that come before nouns.
They may be small, but they make a big difference to meaning.

The **definite article** (the) refers to a specific noun.

Example: The white bear padded through the forest.
(a specific forest previously mentioned)

The **indefinite articles** (a and an) do not refer to specific nouns.

Example: The white bear padded through a forest. (no particular forest)

Articles are not always necessary with plural nouns.

Example: Forests are full of trees.

Focus

1 Choose the correct article (or no article) to go in front of the underlined word.

a Please put your socks in _____ drawer marked socks.

b Please drink _____ glass of milk every morning.

c _____ eggs are laid by hens.

d Give me _____ chance before you close the competition.

e I wore _____ only black trousers in my cupboard.

Practice

2 Revise your word classes.

a _____ conjunctions _____

Words that link words, groups of words or sentences.

b _____

Describe action or a state of being or having something.

c _____

Stand in for nouns to stop repetition.

d _____

A word or group of words used before a noun or pronoun to show place, direction, time, etc.

e _____

Naming words for people, places and things.

f _____

Describe nouns to tell you more about them.

g _____

Give more information about a verb, adjective, phrase, or other adverb; can act as a connective.

h _____

Exclamations or a sudden expression of your feelings (Oh no! Wow!).

nouns
adjectives
verbs
conjunctions
pronouns
adverbs
prepositions
interjections

Challenge

Focus on prepositions.

3   Make a list of all the prepositions you can think of.

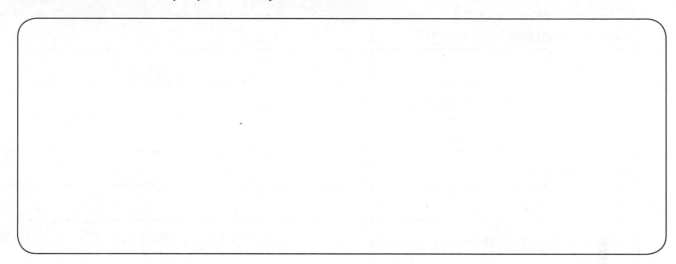

4   Use your list to add the missing vowels to the common prepositions.
    Add new prepositions to your list.

b __tw__ __ n   __ n fr __ nt __ f   thr__ __ gh

__ cr __ ss   b __ s __ d __   __ nd __ r

__ v __ r   b __ l __ w   n__ xt t __

__ b __ v__   __ __ ts __ d __   b __ y __ nd

〉 1.8 Review dialogue

Focus

1   Check your punctuation and reporting words.
    Add the correct punctuation and capital letters, and an interesting alternative to *said*.

a   don't forget to bring your soccer ball tomorrow _____ Javier

b   Ava _____ please may I go to the party – everyone will be there

c   what on earth have you got there _____ Sebastian

d   give me that _____ Nesmah it's mine

Practice

2 Complete the other side of the dialogue.

Youssef	Baba (Dad)
Please may I get one, Baba?	
But why not?	
But I've saved my own money.	
I have got enough – I've checked.	
But I need one.	
That's so unfair.	
Everyone has one now.	
OK, Baba. You're right. I can wait till then.	

Challenge

3 Some word endings sound the same when you say them aloud in dialogue, but they can be spelled differently. Sometimes you just have to learn which ending to use. Choose the correct word ending from the boxes for each word, then check you are right using a dictionary.

–cian   –sion   –ssion   –tion

electri _____   invita _____   techni _____

competi _____   se _____   discu _____

man _____   musi _____   expan _____

4 Write another word with each ending.

_____

_____

_____

_____

> 1.9 Voices

> ## Language focus
>
> **Standard English** is the correct, formal style used in books, newspapers, official documents and business.
>
> Standard English has full sentences, subject–verb agreement, consistent tenses, correct use of word classes and so on.
>
> When we speak, we are not always so formal. We often use idiomatic expressions, abbreviations and contractions in everyday colloquial speech.

Focus

1   Revise standard English. Write **T** (for true) or **F** (for false) at the end of each statement about standard English.

   a   Standard English concerns spelling, grammar and vocabulary. _____

   b   The narrative part of novels is usually written in standard English. _____

   c   Dialogue is always written in standard English. _____

   d   Official documents are written in standard English. _____

   e   Letters or emails to your friends are written in standard English. _____

   f   Reference books and textbooks are not in standard English. _____

   g   The subject and the verb must agree in standard English. _____

   h   Contractions are often used in standard English. _____

   i   In standard English, idioms and colloquialisms should not be used. _____

   j   Standard English means proper sentences and correct punctuation. _____

Practice

2   Tick (✓) the questions and sentences that are written in standard English.

   a Why you looking at that book? ☐

      Why are you looking at that book? ☐

   b I spilt water on my work. ☐

      I spilt water on me work. ☐

   c Martha were over at my house today. ☐

      Martha was over at my house today. ☐

   d You isn't allowed to do that. ☐

      You are not allowed to do that. ☐

   e Me and you make a good team. ☐

      You and I make a good team. ☐

   f Tom and me went to speak to teacher. ☐

      Tom and I went to speak to the teacher. ☐

Challenge

Practise idioms and proverbs.

Idioms and proverbs are both colloquial language, but they are different.
Idioms are groups of words that belong together whose meaning cannot be established from the literal or dictionary meanings of the individual words.
Proverbs are short, wise sayings. The literal meaning is clear, but we infer the lesson from the proverb to apply it in other contexts.

3 Label each sentence as an idiom or a proverb.

   a The early bird catches the worm. _____

   b A bad workman blames his tools. _____

   c My mum is very down to earth. _____

   d One good turn deserves another. _____

   e He's a wolf in sheep's clothing. _____

   f Birds of a feather flock together. _____

   g I am going to go for broke in the last race. _____

4 Choose one of the proverbs from Activity 3.

   a Explain what it means literally.

      _____

   b Explain the lesson that can be learnt from the wise saying.

      _____

      _____

   c Suggest how you could apply the lesson in your own life.

      _____

      _____

> 1.10 Finding out more about flashbacks

Focus

1   Plan a flashback to explain some of the events in this story.
Use the box for your planning.

> **A strange city**
>
> Zahra and Shahid stared at each other. How had they become separated from the
> group? They were in a strange city with no real idea of where they were or how to find
> their group.
>
> 'Shahid,' nudged Zahra anxiously. 'Shahid! Look at everyone. I don't think we did get
> lost – at least not in the way people normally get lost. Look at their clothes, Shahid, and
> the buildings. Where are all the cars? The roads? The noise? And, look! Look at where we
> are. We're still on the temple steps – but they aren't ruins any more – they look new …'

Practice

2   Write a first draft of your flashback.

_____

_____

_____

_____

_____

_____

_____

_____

Challenge

3   Finalise your flashback.

　a   Use a coloured pencil and check your draft for misspelt words
　　　and errors in grammar or punctuation.

　b   Underline any words that could be replaced by more powerful
　　　or descriptive words.

　c   Finally check for flow and sense before rewriting your flashback
　　　with your improvements.

_____

_____

_____

_____

_____

_____

_____

_____

_____

_____

_____

> 1.11 and 1.12 Create Voice 4 at the museum

Focus

1   The noun **perspective** has more than one meaning.
     Write sentences to demonstrate two meanings of *perspective*.

> **Glossary**
>
> **perspective** 1 the way you think about something,
> 2 when things are drawn so that they appear to be
> a realistic size and in a realistic position

a   _____

b   _____

Practice

2   Think about another person's perspective. Rewrite the extract at the beginning
    of Session 1.10 in first-person narrative, from Shahid's perspective.
    Imagine his reaction and what he is thinking.

_____

_____

_____

_____

_____

_____

Challenge

3   What do you think the people thought when they saw Shahid and Zahra?
    What was their perspective on these strange travellers?

    Choose someone who was on the steps and write what they saw from their
    perspective. Make them sound authentic – as if they came from the past.

_____

_____

_____

_____

_____

_____

_____

> 2.1 Making headlines

Language focus

Headlines use a variety of sentence types and punctuation to summarise the news, express a fact and/or an opinion and get the readers' attention. Headline techniques include:

- a statement, question or command
- key words or phrases using well-chosen words to make an impact
- short, simple sentences rather than compound or complex sentences
- active or passive voice for effect.

Focus

1   Use meaningful punctuation to complete these headlines.
    Write each one out in the space provided.

    a   a new season a new team   _____

    b   panic as lights go out   _____

    c   100% vote yes   _____

    d   rain rain go away   _____

    e   is there thyme to cook   _____

Practice

2   Say what you think each headline in Activity 1 means – what the article could be about.

a _____

b _____

c _____

d _____

e _____

Challenge

3   Find three examples of headlines. Write them down.
Make notes to describe their impact using:

• strong words and effective punctuation

• different sentence types

• the active or passive voice.

a _____
_____
_____

b _____
_____
_____

c _____
_____
_____

> 2.2 Read all about it

Focus

1   Underline the fact in each statement and highlight the opinion.
    Rewrite the statement but begin the opinion with the words *I think*.

    a   Punishment is a penalty for wrongdoing and should be used sparingly.

    _____

    _____

    b   There are 24 hours in a day but some days feel too short.

    _____

    c   Vegetables are delicious and they contain lots of vitamins.

    _____

    d   It is good to get up early when the sun rises in the morning.

    _____

    e   Kids should do compulsory sports because exercise makes you fit.

    _____

Practice

2   Write three statements for each topic – a fact, an opinion and a sentence
    that includes both.

School	Climate change
Fact:	Fact:
Opinion:	Opinion:
Both:	Both:

Challenge

3   Circle the word/s in brackets that make each
    sentence have more impact.

    a   He was feeling (*sick* / *unwell*).

    b   She told a (*fib* / *lie*).

    c   Their behaviour was (*bad* / *poor*).

    d   The driver (*crashed* / *bumped*) the car.

    e   The cook (*ruined* / *burnt*) the meat.

    f   The learner was (*naughty* / *mischievous*).

    g   The holiday ended (*suddenly* / *disastrously*).

    h   If you do not study, you might (*fail* / *not pass*).

4   Read about a recent event in your local or international news.
    Write a short summary of it and then complete the following sentences
    to express your opinion about this event.

Summary: _____

_____

_____

a   I think _____

    because _____

b   While some say _____ ,

    I believe _____ .

c   I don't feel _____ ;

    however _____ .

d   Some people agree that _____ ,

    but _____ .

e   Although _____ ,

    I still feel _____ .

> 2.3 Layout and purpose

Language focus

Journalists often describe the structure of a news report as an **inverted** pyramid. This diagram shows how it works. The most important details are included in the first paragraph or **lead**. They answer the 5W1H (Who? What? When? Where? Why? How?) questions. The other details follow. The diagram represents the flow of the information and how important it is, not how much there is.

Most newsworthy information

Who? What? When? Where? Why? How?

Other important details

Optional details

general, background info

Focus

1   Make a list of 'journalist jargon' and write definitions.
    Include words like *lead* or *lede*, *headline*, *byline*, *source*, *inverted pyramid*.

Dictionary

_____

_____

_____

_____

_____

Practice

2   Choose any news article. Read the first paragraph and write 5W1H questions.
    Then answer them.

a   Who?

_____

_____

b   What?

_____

_____

c   Where?

_____

_____

d   When?

_____

_____

e   Why?

_____

_____

f   How? (You may have to look beyond the first paragraph.)

_____

_____

Challenge

3   In your own words, summarise the main events of your article into one sentence.

_____

_____

> 2.4 Report a story

Focus

1 Compare a live news broadcast to a news article. Write notes to describe the purpose, audience, layout and language of a (live) news broadcast, and compare it to a news article. Include these terms:

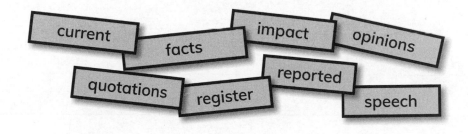

current   facts   impact   opinions   quotations   register   reported   speech

_____

_____

_____

_____

_____

_____

_____

_____

_____

_____

Practice

2   Make a list of criteria to guide a news reporter who reports the news online, on TV or on the radio. What things should they remember to include or do?

Challenge

3   Create and write the lead (the first paragraph) for a live broadcast of a news event. It can be something that has recently happened in your school or local community.

› 2.5 Explore biographies

Focus

1   Use a dictionary to find five words with the prefix *bio*.
    Write the words and the definitions.

a   _____

b   _____

c   _____

d   _____

e   _____

Practice

2   Read a biography and <u>underline</u> the facts. Make notes on the next page using a mind
    map and key words.

Poorna Malavath

Poorna Malavath is a brave young girl who believes that with confidence and
focus you can achieve anything, no matter who you are. She is a true example
because she is the youngest person in the world to summit Mount Everest.

At the age of 13 when most children are at school, playing
games or watching TV, she had her eyes fixed on making a
difference in her community and changing the views of society.
Her story is an inspiration to anyone from any background,
young and old.

On 10 June 2000, Poorna Malavath was born in a small village
in India where her parents worked on a farm. She attended the
local school that taught mountain climbing as a subject. This
sparked her desire to take up the ultimate challenge – to climb
Mount Everest, a mountain on which many lives have been lost.

Challenge

3   Read a biography of someone else. Write a short summary of this person.

_____

_____

_____

_____

_____

_____

_____

❯ 2.6 and 2.7 Make a start

Language focus

A **relative pronoun** takes the place of a noun and acts as a connective. It connects a clause or phrase to a noun that has already been mentioned. The clause or phrase modifies or adds more information to that noun. Relative pronouns are placed directly after the noun they modify. They can also join sentences.

There are five main relative pronouns:

- who, whom, whose and which refer to people
- that and which refer to animals or objects.

Example: This is the girl <u>who</u> climbed Mount Everest.

This is the mountain <u>that</u> she climbed.

The pronoun which is usually preceded by a preposition.

Focus

1 Say who or what the <u>underlined</u> pronouns refer to.

a The children love the apples you bought from the seller. <u>They</u> are delicious.

_____

b The interviewer asked the children questions. <u>He</u> wasn't sure who answered <u>them</u> first.

_____

c The guides saw the climbers leave the camp. Some went missing but <u>they</u> found <u>them</u>.

_____

d This is the brave girl <u>whose</u> name was mentioned in the paper for <u>her</u> brave deed.

_____

e I am proud of <u>myself</u> and my team for achieving the goals <u>we</u> set.

_____

f The young climber is famous. <u>This</u> is the school that <u>she</u> went to.

_____

Practice

2 Use the biographical timeline to write five full sentences
in the past tense.

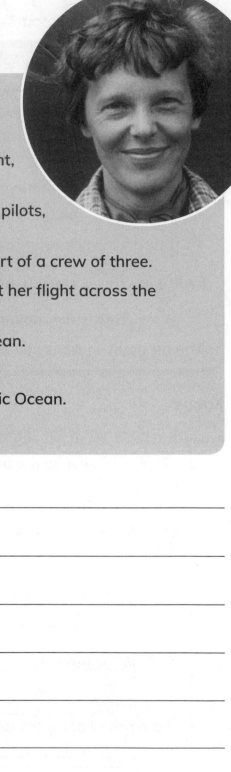

Amelia Earhart

1897 (24 July): Born in a small town in Kansas, USA.

1921: Learnt to fly and bought her first plane, a bright,
yellow biplane named *The Canary*.

1922: Achieved the world altitude record for women pilots,
14 000 ft (4267 m).

1928: First woman to cross the Atlantic Ocean as part of a crew of three.

1928: Published her first book, *20 Hrs. 40 Min.*, about her flight across the
Atlantic Ocean.

1932: First woman to fly solo across the Atlantic Ocean.

1932: First person to cross the Atlantic Ocean twice.

1937 (2 July): Went missing in a plane over the Pacific Ocean.

1939 (5 January): Declared dead.

_____

_____

_____

_____

_____

_____

_____

Challenge

3   Plan a biography about Amelia Earhart or any adult in your school or community. Do further research or conduct an interview to gather information and then write three paragraphs with headings. Use the headings provided or make up your own.

Early life

_____

_____

_____

Training and career

_____

_____

_____

Achievements

_____

_____

_____

_____

> 2.8 Another life

Focus

1   Use a dictionary to find five words with the prefix auto.
    Write the word and the definition.

a _____

b _____

c _____

d _____

e _____

Practice

2   Compare the features of an autobiography and a biography.
    Use this table. Write auto, bio or both next to each feature.

1 A written account of another person's life		6 It describes the context, e.g. time period, peers, culture, world view and historical setting.	
2 It uses first-person narrative with pronouns *I, me, we.*		7 A personal account (includes memoirs and journals)	
3 It uses third-person narrative with pronouns *he, she, they.*		8 The 'voice' is not the voice of the subject.	
4 The style is subjective: events are told from the subject's point of view.		9 The 'voice' is the voice of the subject.	
5 The style is objective: the writer expresses points of view based on other sources.		10 A written account of a person's life, written by that person	

Challenge

3 Plan an autobiography. It can be your own or you can choose to write as someone else.

- Draw a timeline to mark special events.
- Choose an interesting title and introduction.
- Describe your family and friends.
- Write about a specific event or incident that others might enjoy reading.

My timeline:

Title

_____

Introduction

_____

_____

_____

_____

Family and friends

_____

_____

_____

_____

_____

_____

_____

_____

_____

_____

An event

_____

_____

_____

_____

> ## 2.9 Conduct an interview

Focus

1 If you wanted to find out about someone, what six questions would you ask them? Write them out.

a _____

b _____

c _____

d _____

e _____

f _____

Practice

2   Use your questions to interview a friend or someone
    in your family. Write the answers here.

a   _____

b   _____

c   _____

d   _____

e   _____

f   _____

Challenge

3   List five criteria to guide an interview. What should you do or not do?

> 2.10 Practise reporting

Language focus

When you change from **direct speech** to **indirect speech**, the following things change:

- The punctuation changes as you remove the inverted commas.

- The verbs change from present tense to past tense.
  (The future forms *will* and *going to* change to *would* or *was going to*.)

- Pronouns change. (*I* to *he* or *she*; *we* to *they*; *you* to *him*, *her*, *us* or *them*)

- Adverbs of time change. (*Yesterday* to *the day before*; *Tomorrow* to *the following day*).

- The reported speech is often introduced by *that*.

Focus

1   Rewrite the following sentences with the correct punctuation.
    Show the quotation in speech marks.

   a   I had an amazing experience she told the interviewer when she returned.

   _____

   _____

   b   A classmate said of her friend she is brave and focused and a wonderful friend.

   _____

   _____

   c   The children chanted she's our hero as they gathered to greet her.

   _____

   _____

   d   Her parents commented we are overjoyed and very proud of her.

   _____

   _____

   e   The headline welcome home filled the front page.

   _____

Practice

2   Complete the sentences in reported speech.
    Remove the punctuation and change the words in **bold**.

a   Everyone said 'We are ready to go.'

    Everyone said that _____

    _____

b   'Our adventure began yesterday,' she declared.

    She declared that _____

    _____

c   'You must complete the homework by tomorrow,' the
    teacher told the children.

    The teacher told the children that _____

    _____

d   'You should pack your bags for school,' the
    mother told her son.

    The mother told her son that _____

    _____

Challenge

3   Find examples in a news article of reported speech.
    Write out five sentences from the article.

a   _____

b   _____

c   _____

d   _____

e   _____

> 2.11 and 2.12 Write a news article

Focus

1   Plan a news report about someone who did something great – recently or in history. Research the event and make notes. Include facts and opinions.

Practice

2 Organise the information into sections.
Think about the inverted pyramid. Plan a rough draft.

Headline _____

_____

_____

Lead _____

_____

_____

Less important _____

_____

_____

Least important _____

_____

_____

Challenge

3 Write the article out neatly in the template provided. Use the checklist to guide you.
You can include a picture of the person.

The report has an attention-grabbing headline.	
The lead answers all the question words.	
The report includes mainly facts and some opinion.	
The report is written mainly in the past tense.	
The report includes a few quotations, correctly punctuated.	
The style and tone of the report is formal and impersonal.	
The language used is correct.	
The report is edited and has been proofread.	

3 > Personification and imagery

> 3.1 *The River*

> **Language focus**
>
> **Personification** is a poetic device – a type of figurative language that poets use to create images in a reader's mind. It means giving human feelings and actions to objects or ideas.

Focus

1   Circle the examples of personification.

The box was wrapped up and tied with a pretty ribbon.	The washing machine coughed and spluttered before stopping.
The sun beamed as it tiptoed its way across the sky.	The window flung itself open and breathed in the fresh air.
The icicle shivered and its teeth chattered.	The mice crept about like soft toys.

The tree was a gallant soldier.

Practice

2   Write sentences to personify these objects.

    a   **teapot:** _____

    b   **carrot:** _____

    c   **flower:** _____

    d   **bath tub:** _____

    e   **cave:** _____

Challenge

3   Write a one-stanza poem containing at least one example of personification.

_____

_____

_____

_____

_____

› 3.2 Compare poems

Mood is the feeling or atmosphere a poem creates. Poets create mood by using imagery, figurative language, rhyme and rhythm. If the mood changes in a poem, it is signalled by a change in the way the words are used; for example, long drawn-out sounds could be followed by short, hard sounds.

Focus

1 Use the adjectives in boxes to describe mood.
Put them in the table under the mood you think they belong to.

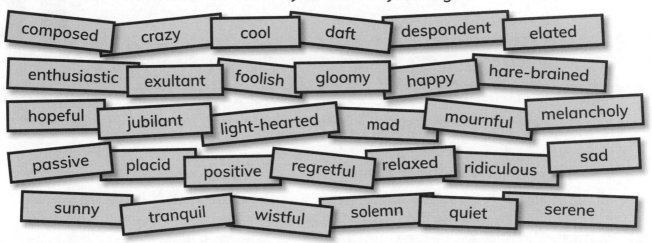

optimism	silliness	sadness	peace

Practice

2 Read the stanza.

> Over the winter glaciers
>
> I see the summer glow,
>
> And through the wild-piled snowdrift
>
> The warm rosebuds below.
>
> *Ralph Waldo Emerson*

A glacier is a large mass of ice that moves very slowly, down a slope or valley.

a   Answer the questions.

• What is the poem about? _____

_____

• Explain if it is winter or summer: _____

_____

- How does the poem make you feel? Choose a word to describe its mood.

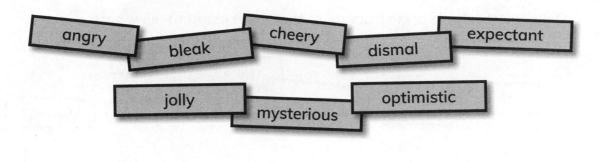

angry   bleak   cheery   dismal   expectant   jolly   mysterious   optimistic

_____

- Explain why you chose your word. _____

_____

_____

_____

b   Are the sounds of the words sharp and hard, long and soft or changing?

_____

_____

c   Explain how the sounds of the words support your choice of mood.

_____

_____

Challenge

3   Describe the structure and features of the poem in Activity 2.

   a   Describe the form and structure of the poem using these words:

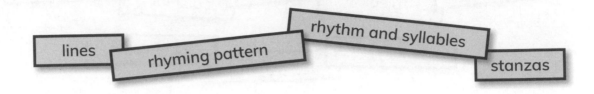

lines

rhyming pattern

rhythm and syllables

stanzas

_____

_____

   b   Find the rhyming words in line 3. _____

   c   What is unusual about their position? _____

> ## 3.3 Look deeper

Focus

1   a   Read the traditional nursery rhyme.

> ### Jack and Jill
>
> Jack and Jill went up the hill
>
> To fetch a pail of water;
>
> Jack fell down and broke his crown,
>
> And Jill came tumbling after.

- The nursery rhyme has a strong rhythm. Describe the pattern of beats using DUM for stressed syllables and de for unstressed syllables. The first line has been started.
- Write in the number of syllables at the end of each line.

DUM de DUM _____ _____

_____ _____

_____ _____

_____ _____

b   What feeling does this rhythm give you? What is the mood of the rhyme?

_____

Practice

2   Poets use rhyming words in several different ways:

- Rhymes at the end of lines are called **end rhymes**.
- Rhymes in the middle of a line are called **internal rhymes**.
- Words that almost rhyme are called **half rhymes**.

Describe how each rhyming pattern is used (if at all) in the nursery rhyme in Activity 1. Give examples.

a   End rhymes: _____

b   Internal rhymes: _____

c   Half rhymes: _____

Challenge

3   Word sounds are very important for creating mood in poems.
    Poets use **alliteration** and **onomatopoeia** to create special sound effects.

    Read the poems and complete the poem notes.

    a   Write the correct words on top of the definitions.

    b   Draw lines joining the examples to the correct poem notes.
        (Hint: They might belong to both notes.)

1   Cunningly creeping, a
    spectral stalker.

2   It SHUSHES
    It hushes
    The loudness in the road.
    It flitter-twitters,
    And laughs away from me.

3   How many cookies could a
    good cook cook if a good cook
    could cook cookies? A good
    cook could cook as much
    cookies as a good cook who
    could cook cookies.

4   Over the cobbles he clattered and clashed in the dark inn-yard.
    He tapped with his whip on the shutters, but all was locked and barred;
    ...
    Tlot tlot, tlot tlot! Had they heard it? The horse-hooves, ringing clear;
    Tlot tlot, tlot tlot, in the distance! Were they deaf that they did not hear?

Poem notes

Using words that include
sounds that are similar to the
noises the words refer to.

Poem notes

Using words, especially in poetry,
of the same sound or sounds,
especially consonants, at the
beginning of several words that
are close together.

〉 3.4 Right Here Was the Ocean

Focus

1   Revise personification.
Choose the correct words from the boxes to complete the text.

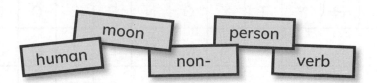

Personification means using _____ qualities or actions to describe a

_____ living object. The word *personification* is a clue because it contains

the word _____ . Personify is a _____ meaning describe

something as if it were a person. So, rather than saying: *The moon is a crescent shape*

tonight, say: *The _____ is just peeping out tonight.*

Practice

2   More about personification.
Choose the correct words from the boxes to complete the text.

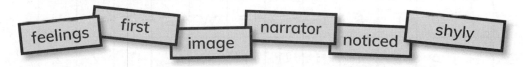

Using a human word to describe an object makes a poetic _____ more

vivid. It can also tell you how the _____ of the poem feels about the

object. For example, *The moon _____ watched me*, shows sympathy

with the moon; whereas, *The moon barely _____ me* does not show

sympathy. Poems can also be written in _____ person as if the object

has _____ like a person.

Challenge

3 Complete the figurative language wordsearch.

Z	R	S	T	A	N	Z	A	T	R	Z	A	O	H
N	S	O	A	H	R	T	I	H	A	P	L	N	S
M	M	T	I	H	Y	T	Y	O	N	R	L	O	E
A	E	P	Y	R	R	M	A	M	O	E	I	M	H
O	S	T	P	E	E	A	L	Y	I	S	T	A	R
Y	H	H	A	I	A	N	N	E	T	S	E	T	E
M	E	A	A	P	S	A	I	E	I	N	R	O	A
R	N	Y	M	P	H	O	T	C	T	R	A	P	R
S	I	M	I	L	E	O	R	N	E	O	T	O	L
I	R	N	P	T	I	Y	R	S	P	I	I	E	M
E	C	N	A	N	O	S	S	A	E	H	O	I	N
M	S	R	T	Y	T	E	M	S	R	A	N	A	O
A	D	Y	A	L	P	D	R	O	W	S	P	O	N
M	O	H	A	E	I	N	O	T	A	E	T	Z	Z

ALLITERATION RHYTHM
ASSONANCE SHAPE
METAPHOR SIMILE
ONOMPATOPOEIA STANZA
REPETITION WORDPLAY
RHYME

> 3.5 Explore figurative language

Language focus

A **metaphor** is a figure of speech where a word or a phrase is used to describe something as if it were something else. It compares two normally unrelated things.

Example: Jamal is a real brick. *(Jamal is obviously not a brick, but it is a good way to describe his solid characteristics as a friend.)*

An **extended metaphor** is a metaphorical comparison that continues in a series of sentences in a paragraph or lines in a poem.

Example: Jamal is a real brick. He has <u>laid the foundation</u> of a good friendship. He is the <u>building block</u> on which we all depend.

Focus

1 Identify the extended metaphor.

   a <u>Underline</u> the words and phrases that make up the extended metaphor.

   The tide of life ebbs and flows. It sings when life is good. It cries when times are bad.

   b Continue the extended metaphor for one more line.

   _____

Practice

2 Write three metaphors to describe **a motorway**.

   _____

   _____

   _____

Challenge

3   Use your metaphors in a short, illustrated poem titled **The Motorway**.

Include the following in your poem:

- your three metaphors to create an extended metaphor
- one simile
- some rhyme (end, internal or half rhyme).

_____

_____

_____

_____

> 3.6 Write your own poem

Focus

1   Generate a word web. Prepare to write a poem about a windy night by creating some word webs of interesting descriptive words and synonyms. Use a thesaurus or online tool to help you find words.

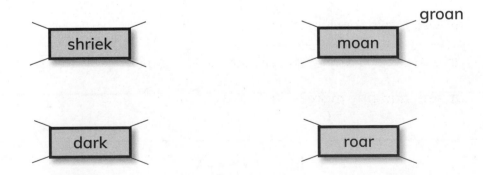

Practice

2   Write a first draft of your poem.

- Include figurative language to increase the visual impact of your poem.

- Include any poetic techniques that will increase the impact of your poem.

_____

_____

_____

_____

_____

_____

_____

Challenge

3   Edit and improve your poem from Activity 2.

a   Underline any words you think you could find more descriptive or powerful alternatives for and use a thesaurus to replace them.

b   Review your figurative language.

- Can you make it more effective?

- Can you extend any of the metaphors?

- Can you add any more?

c   Review your poetic techniques and structure.

- Can you change the line lengths to create an effect?

- Can you change the structure of the stanzas?

- Can you add rhyme or create a clear rhythm?

- Can you include any alliteration or onomatopoeia?

d   Write out a final version of your poem as creatively as possible and illustrate it.

_____

_____

_____

_____

_____

_____

_____

4 ▶ Back to the future

⟩ 4.1 Looking into the future

Focus

1 English contains words from many languages.

   a Voyager in French is the verb to *travel* and voyage in French means *journey*.
   Use this knowledge of word origins to explain the meaning of the words
   voyage and voyager in English.

   _____

   _____

   b Use each word in a sentence to show you know what they mean.

   _____

   _____

Practice

Explore word origins and spelling.

Did you know that up to 30 percent of English words originate from French?

2 Read the words in the boxes. They are all words that English borrows from French.

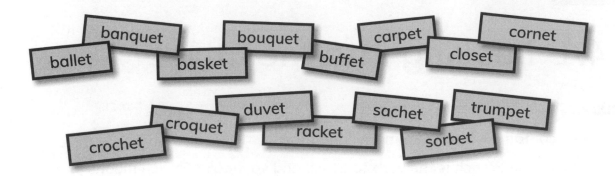

a Identify the common word endings.

_____

b Say each word to yourself and then write each one on the correct notice board.

THEY NOTICE BOARD	EDIT NOTICE BOARD
et sounds the same as ey, as in they	et sounds the same as it, as in edit

3 Try to find more words ending in –et to add to your notice boards.

4   Choose five words borrowed from French from your lists and use them in sentences.

_____

_____

_____

_____

_____

Challenge

Many words that are used in music have Italian origins. We call these words jargon or technical language because they are specific to a particular activity or job.

5   Match the musical words to their meanings.

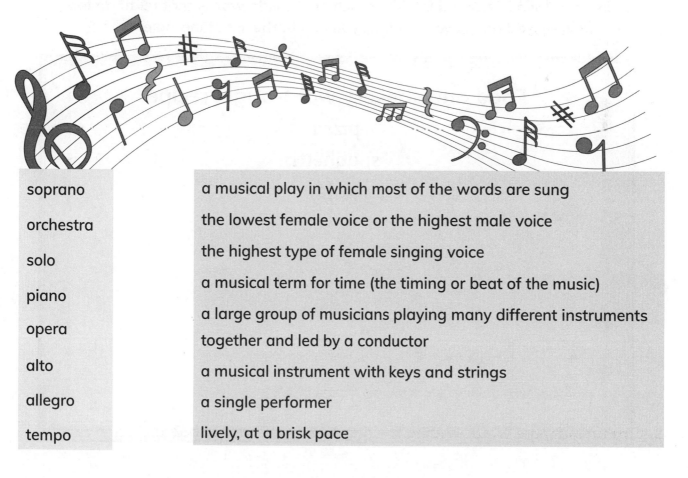

soprano	a musical play in which most of the words are sung
orchestra	the lowest female voice or the highest male voice
solo	the highest type of female singing voice
piano	a musical term for time (the timing or beat of the music)
opera	a large group of musicians playing many different instruments together and led by a conductor
alto	a musical instrument with keys and strings
allegro	a single performer
tempo	lively, at a brisk pace

Some of these words have other meanings and uses too — like *solo*. You can check the word origins using an etymological dictionary.

6   Which letters do the words in Activity 5 end in? _____

7   Lots of words ending in o, a and *i* have Italian origins.
    Can you think of any others?

    _____

    _____

8   English has also borrowed lots of French and Italian words that relate to food
    and cooking. Add as many words as you can to the list of ingredients.

Food and cookery word-origin recipe

pizza

spaghetti

café

> 4.2 Step into their shoes

Focus

1   If you were visiting a remote area with no electricity for a week and you had to pack everything in a backpack, what would you take?

   a   First, make a mind map of everything you think you might need. Use key words.

Mind map of what I might need on my wilderness trip:

Make sure that you can take everything in one backpack — remember you have to carry it!

b   Decide what you would take in order of importance.
     Write three separate lists, using commas to separate your list items.

     Essential items: _____

     _____

     Useful but inessential items: _____

     _____

     Luxuries (nice to have): _____

     _____

Practice

Nouns that end in –ance can form adjectives ending in –ant.
Nouns that end in –ence can form adjectives ending in –ent.

2   Write the related adjective for each noun.

a   elegance   _____   g   tolerance   _____

b   absence   _____   h   confidence   _____

c   importance   _____   i   ignorance   _____

d   adolescence   _____   j   presence   _____

e   magnificence   _____   k   brilliance   _____

f   significance   _____   l   dependence   _____

Challenge

Some nouns related to –*ant* and –*ent* words take the endings –*ancy* or –*ency* if they refer to a quality or a state of being, e.g. *infant* ⟶ *infancy*: the state of being an infant.

3 Predict how these nouns will be spelled with the suffixes –*ancy* and –*ency*.

a accountant _____

b consistent _____

c truant _____

d tenant _____

e fluent _____

f frequent _____

g efficient _____

h buoyant _____

i transparent _____

j lenient _____

> 4.3 Useful punctuation and grammar tips

Language focus

Pairs of brackets, dashes or **commas** enclose a word or words to separate them from the main sentence. The words in parenthesis can be:

- an explanation
  Example: Cairo (the capital city of Egypt) is near the Nile delta.
- additional information
  Example: Mount Elbrus in Russia, at 5642 metres, is the highest mountain in Europe.
- an aside or afterthought
  Example: I watched the match – which was brilliant – before going to bed.

Focus

1 Brackets, dashes and commas can be useful.
Put **parentheses** into these sentences to
separate a group of words from the main sentence.

> **Key word**
>
> **parentheses:** brackets, dashes or commas

    a   I take part in two sports basketball and golf that require lots of practice.

    b   The learners who are only in Year 6 have set up their own business.

    c   The Dead Sea in fact a hypersaline lake is one of the world's saltiest bodies of water.

    d   Homework although I hate doing it helps me be an independent learner.

    e   My holiday in Greece my best holiday ever was almost three years ago.

Practice

2 Rewrite this email to a friend using parentheses to add additional information or asides to make the email more personal and informal.

> It's the holidays (finally) ! We're going to stay with our cousins on the coast. I am hoping to go snorkelling if the weather's good enough. I can't believe we won't be back at school for six whole weeks. Dad says the holidays are too long and that I should do some work in them! See you next term.

In formal writing, don't use brackets unless you have to. Too many brackets look like you didn't plan before you started writing.

Challenge

Language focus

Quantifiers are words that modify a noun to answer the question *How much?* without giving an exact answer. Quantifiers are words like *all, most, many, more, some, none, few, fewer, less, both, no, enough, some, each* and *every*. Some **quantifiers** are singular, some are plural and some may be either.

* Use a plural verb when you modify a countable noun with one of the following quantifiers: *all, most, many, some, few, fewer, both.*

* Use a singular verb when you have an uncountable (mass) noun: *less, enough, no.*

3   Quantifiers need to agree with the verb.
    Choose the correct verbs to match the quantifiers in these sentences.

   a   Neither of the learners is / are able to answer the question.

   b   Few of the matches is / are won easily.

   c   Less sugar is / are better for your health.

   d   Most of the houses has / have water-saving devices these days.

   e   No mud was / were found in the house.

4   Choose a suitable quantifier to complete the sentences.

    a   There are _____ birds nesting in the trees than last year. [less, fewer, many]

    b   I must put _____ salt than usual in the cooking to be healthy. [less, fewer, most]

    c   _____ entrant has to complete the whole cross-country course to qualify.
       [each, several, more]

    d   _____ girls decided to go to the movies rather than go ice-skating.
       [both, every, each]

    e   _____ effort has been put in to make the event worthwhile.
       [both, enough, fewer]

> 4.4 Begin planning a longer story

Focus

1   Read the summaries of the seven chapters in *The Green Book* by Jill Paton Walsh.
    Note: the chapter summaries are not in the order according to the book.

    a   What tense are they written in? _____

    b   Give some examples of verbs in this tense. _____

    c   What is the effect of using this tense? _____

Chapter _____

After four years, their spaceship arrives and touches down. The voyagers explore the strange landscape, test the water, breathe the air, and find out if they can eat the plants and grow their seeds. The plants are like glass, sharp and shiny like jewels and easily broken. But the lake is more inviting. Pattie, as the youngest traveller, names the planet _Shine_.

Chapter _____

Life on the new planet is difficult and boring with little to do but wait to see if the crops will grow. The crops are not a success and everyone worries about food stores running out, especially when the rabbits die too. Things look up when the children discover trees oozing a sweet gooey and edible candy.

Chapter _____

Early on, the children go for a picnic in Boulder Valley but while they are there, the boulders crack open and gigantic _moth people_ fly out, terrifying everyone. Pattie offers a pot of the candy in friendship to the **moth people** who turn out to be friendly. The voyagers' wheat crop grows but is brittle, with glassy, hexagonal seeds. People begin to worry once more about how to survive.

Chapter _____

Father, Joe, Sarah and Pattie pack for their four-year journey to escape the Disaster on Earth and begin their new life on a distant planet. Once on board, the children share their books but they laugh at Pattie's choice of a blank, green notebook. The children begin to worry about whether the new planet will be able to sustain life.

Chapter _____

Everyone is overjoyed when the children are fine; they realise they will be able to live on the strange, glassy wheat crop. Father turns the old moth wings into thread to make clothes. Slowly, the people realise they have a future after all. Joe finds Pattie's green book which is now full of writing. Father reads it out to everybody – it is the story of the people of Shine.

Chapter _____

Only the children have time to play and explore while adults build the village and plough the land to plant seeds. Pattie and Joe find a valley full of huge, perfectly round boulders. When the people try to cook and eat the bright green jellyfish, they turn out to be a good fuel to burn for light. Father decides to make practical gadgets to help the colony survive.

Chapter _____

Pattie sees the moth people gather together for a strange dance before flying off over the lake. The next day only a few moth people make it back swollen, heavy and dying as they crawl into Boulder Valley. Father explains that these moths will be the next generation once they hatch. Sarah grinds up the hard beads of wheat into a powder and makes bread to share with her sister and brother. Father worries that they will die as if they'd eaten glass.

2 a Rewrite the first summary in Activity 1 in the past tense.

_____

_____

_____

_____

_____

_____

_____

_____

b Explain how this changes the effect.

_____

_____

_____

Practice

3 Order the chapters in Activity 1.

    a Order the chapters by writing the correct chapter number at the top of each summary.

    b Rewrite the final chapter summary (Chapter 7) in the future tense.

_____

_____

_____

_____

_____

_____

_____

_____

Challenge

4 Think of a suitable title for each chapter and draw up a contents page using
this space. Estimate the page numbers based on your experience
of book length. Illustrate the contents page to reflect the storyline.

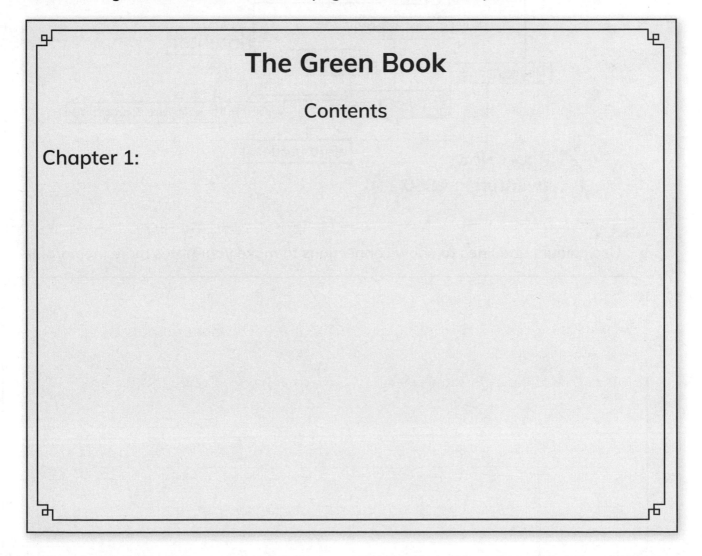

The Green Book

Contents

Chapter 1:

> 4.5 Going back and looking into the future

Focus

Jules Verne, a famous science-fiction writer who was sometimes known as the 'father' of science fiction, was writing around 1850. Research everyday things we might take for granted today that were not invented when he was writing.

1   a   Make notes on a mind map using key words – like the example.

Example:

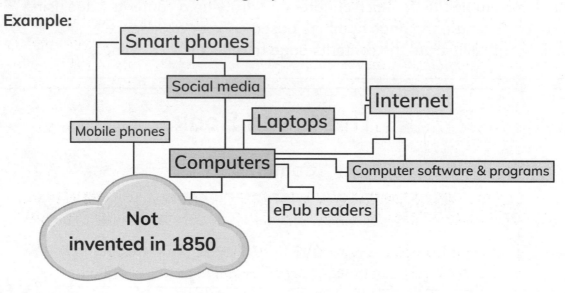

b   Use colours and lines to show connections to make your notes more memorable.

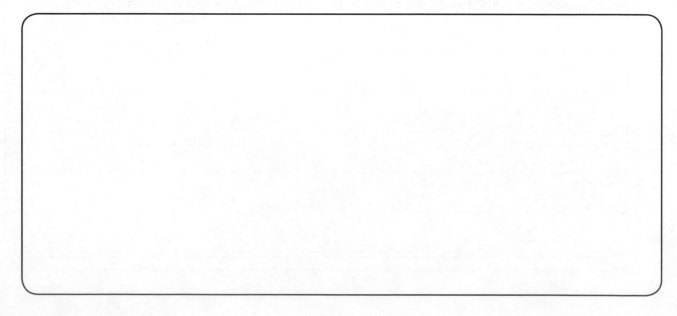

Practice

2   Use your own words. Skim the paragraph from Jules Verne's story *Journey to the Interior of the Earth* and summarise the main idea in one sentence.

_____

_____

> *On their journey to the interior of the Earth, Axel and his uncle, Professor Leidenbrock, encounter a gigantic, subterranean sea. Axel realises the light cannot be coming from the sun.*
>
> If my eyes were able to range afar over this great sea, it was because a peculiar light brought to view every detail of it. It was not the light of the sun, with his dazzling shafts of brightness and the splendour of his rays; nor was it the pale and uncertain shimmer of the moonbeams, the dim reflection of a nobler body of light. No; the illuminating power of this light, its trembling diffusiveness, its bright, clear whiteness, and its low temperature, showed that it must be of electric origin. It was like an **aurora borealis**, a continuous *cosmical* phenomenon, filling a cavern of sufficient extent to contain an ocean.

Glossary

aurora borealis: a natural light display in the sky caused by charged particles colliding with atoms in the atmosphere

3   Explain where the light is coming from if it *cannot be coming from the sun.*

_____

_____

_____

_____

_____

_____

Challenge

Read the questions and then scan the main paragraph in Activity 2 to answer them.

4 a Axel first describes what the light is not like. Which sentence describes what the light is like?

_____

b *Cosmical* is an old-fashioned word. What form would you use today?

_____

5 *Subterranean* originates from Latin.
Use the diagram to explain how the word is formed in English.

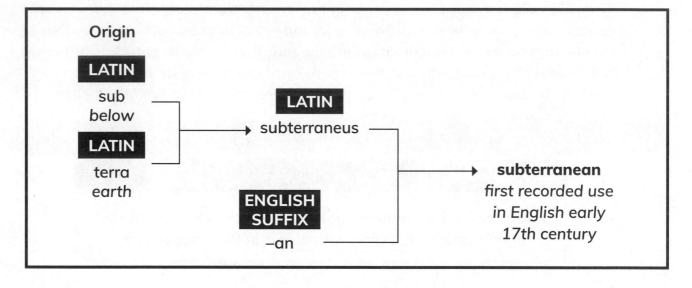

_____

_____

_____

_____

_____

_____

_____

6 Rewrite this extract in your own words. You do not have to change it word for word. Read it, understand it and then write just the main idea in your own words.

> It was not the light of the sun, with his dazzling shafts of brightness and the splendour of his rays; nor was it the pale and uncertain shimmer of the moonbeams, the dim reflection of a nobler body of light.

_____

_____

_____

_____

> 4.6 Working with voices and moods

Language focus

The **active voice** is when the subject does the action to someone or something:

Example: Giovanni rode the bike.
                 ↑   ↑   ↑
              subject + active + direct
                        verb   object

The **passive voice** is when the subject has the action done to it:

Example: The bike was ridden by Giovanni.
                 ↑   ↑   ↑   ↖
              subject + passive + preposition + agent
                        verb

Passive verbs have a 'helping' verb (_to be_) + past participle:

Example: The bag <u>was dropped</u>. The clothes <u>are damaged</u>.

The 'helping' verb agrees with the subject and indicates the tense: past, present or future.

The main verb appears as the past participle:

Examples: dropped, damaged, blown

Focus

1 a Circle the correct heading for each column.

   b Match the active form to the passive form of each sentence.

	Active / Passive
a	Axel picked up a fossil.
b	Axel carried the lantern in his hand.
c	Axel told a story to the others.
d	Axel checked the direction on the compass.
e	The professor told Axel to point towards north.
f	Axel stared at the bright, peculiar light.

	Active / Passive
i	The others were told a story by Axel.
ii	The direction was checked on the compass by Axel.
iii	A fossil was picked up by Axel.
iv	The bright, peculiar light was stared at by Axel.
v	The lantern was carried by Axel in his hand.
vi	Axel was told to point towards north by the professor.

Practice

2 Change the sentences from passive to active voice.

   a The food is always prepared by the family.

_____

   b The ball was given to the best player by the coach.

_____

   c The street will be decorated for the festival by the children.

_____

   d Several science-fiction novels were written by Jules Verne.

_____

   e The can of tomatoes was opened by the chef.

_____

Language focus

To make a sentence passive, search for the subject and make it do the action.

Example: The cars were designed → Motor Cars Ltd
by Motor Cars Ltd.   designed the cars.

3   Change the sentences from active to passive voice.

a   The sun gave off a warm, glowing heat.

_____

b   The teacher checked the learners' uniforms for tidiness.

_____

c   The dog chewed the stick into pieces.

_____

d   The nurse washed the boy's wound gently.

_____

e   Several riders patted the horses after the race.

_____

Challenge

4   Rewrite the passage in the opposite mood.

Axel dug a hole in the sand. His jacket was folded by the Professor up on a nearby boulder to stay dry. Axel's spade struck something hard, making a metal on metal sound. Quickly the hole was cleared by the Professor and Axel with their hands. Axel picked up the object slowly and carefully. They both stared at it, saying nothing at first. Suddenly the object started to give off a faint glow and a low hum…

_____

_____

_____

_____

_____

> 4.7 Working with chapters, paragraphs and connectives

Focus

Connectives have various purposes in linking parts of a sentence, for example: **sequencing, comparing, adding, contrasting** or **cause and effect**.

1 <u>Underline</u> the connective in each sentence and write its purpose at the end.

   Example: Amélie was excited <u>because</u> it was her birthday. <u>cause and effect</u>

   a   He ate breakfast before he went to school. _____

   b   We couldn't decide what to do so we went to bed. _____

   c   I didn't understand my homework although I tried my hardest. _____

   d   Misha packed carefully so that everything would fit. _____

   e   The learners left the class as soon as the bell rang. _____

Practice

2 Complete these multi-clause sentences and <u>underline</u> the connectives.

   a   The exam was hard but _____

   b   Although it was hot, _____

   c   Jamal finished before _____

   d   While the boys went to the shops, _____

   e   Despite working hard, _____

Challenge

3   Join these sentences choosing a suitable connective from the boxes.

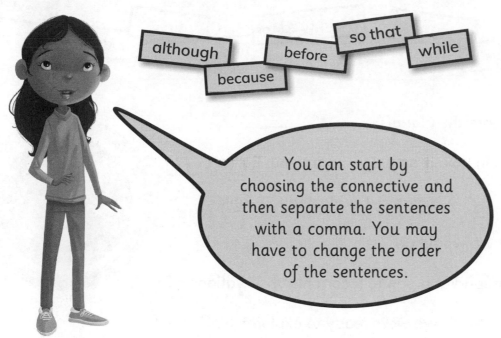

although   before   so that   while

because

You can start by choosing the connective and then separate the sentences with a comma. You may have to change the order of the sentences.

a   Prahlad wasn't worried. He did not anticipate trouble.

_____

b   Professor Shonku packed what he needed for the mission. He went down to Mars.

_____

c   An unusual thing happened. I was writing in my diary.

_____

d   I sat down. I would not be tired.

_____

e   I trusted my assistant. I didn't believe he would be able to help me.

_____

4 Complete the passage with suitable connectives from the boxes.
You may need to start some of the connectives with capital letters.

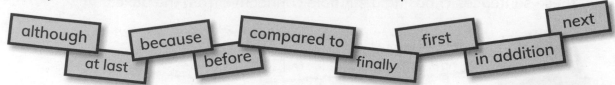

although   because   compared to   first   next
at last   before   finally   in addition

I wanted to explore the planet _____

I was interested in how it would compare with Earth.

_____ I started, I explained to Prahlad

everything that we would do. _____

I gave him a notepad and pen to record his observations.

_____, we were ready to explore.

_____, we tested the ground and the rocks, which seemed to be quite

soft. _____, we drank the red river water _____ not

without some nervousness. _____, we made sketches of the plants,

noting they were blue _____ the green we were used to on Earth.

> 4.8 Write paragraphs describing fictional surroundings

Focus

1 Jules Verne, the science-fiction writer, was writing over 150 years ago and his writing
can sound a little old-fashioned. Underline all the words in this passage that you think
you could replace to make the writing seem more old-fashioned.

These are really odd flowers. Their smell is so strong that I smelled the flowers long before I could see them. The colours are so bright – too bright – and yet I can't look away from them. They are amazing to look at.

Practice

2   Rewrite the passage in Activity 1 using an old-fashioned style like Jules Verne's. Use the *Old-fashioned word bank* to help you.

Imagine you are speaking in an old-fashioned way. Writers often used lots of extra words in the old days – see if you can too! Use your dictionary to look up any words you don't yet know.

Old-fashioned word bank

incongruous, idiosyncratic, uncommon, out of the usual way, bouquet, aroma, overwhelming, exotic, arresting, prodigious, awe-inspiring, potent, overwhelming, pungent, became aware of, sensed, nasal awareness, some considerable time, in advance, afore, prior to, vision, hues, shades, tints, vivid, intense, dazzling, hypnotised, remove my gaze, direct my contemplation, elsewhere, behold

_____

_____

_____

Challenge

3   Write your own old-fashioned paragraph about something else you found on the expedition. Use the *Old-fashioned word bank* to help you.

_____

_____

_____

> 4.9 Going forward in time

Focus

1   Complete the passage with suitable time connectives from the boxes.

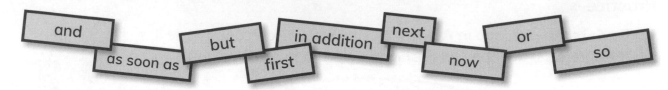

What a strange day I have had a _____ that I look back on it.

b _____ I woke up, I knew something was up. c _____,

there were no complaints d _____ moans from my sisters.

e _____, the bathroom was empty f _____ I dashed in

g _____ bolted the door. h _____, I stepped into the

shower i _____ this was no shower I had ever seen before ...

Practice

2   Continue the extract in Activity 1 for another paragraph. Include the following
    time connectives:

_____

_____

_____

_____

_____

_____

Challenge

3   The year is 2166. Write your own beginning to a science-fiction story.
Make sure you include features that tell readers that they are starting
to read a science-fiction tale. Use time connectives to link your
clauses and sentences.

_____

_____

_____

_____

_____

_____

_____

> 4.10 Spelling, punctuation and grammar

Focus

–ible or *–able*?

1   Choose the correct suffix (*–ible* or *–able*) to add to the following word roots.

a   incred _____   d   fashion _____   g   size _____

b   unsupport _____   e   desir _____   h   flex _____

c   vis _____   f   leg _____   i   respons _____

2   Choose three of the words to use in sentences.

a   _____

b   _____

c   _____

Practice

3   Choose the correct suffix (–or or –er) to complete these words to create agent nouns.

a   act_____   g   edit_____

b   sail_____   h   danc_____

c   work_____   i   runn_____

d   build_____   j   driv_____

e   tut_____   k   invent_____

f   dictat_____   l   surviv_____

4   Choose three of the agent nouns to use in sentences.

a   _____

b   _____

c   _____

Challenge

5   Choose the correct suffix (–er or –or) for each word and then find the words in the wordsearch.

Suffixes

convert	_____	lov	_____
elig	_____	revers	_____
inspect	_____	survey	_____
leg	_____	direct	_____
notice	_____	govern	_____
suggest	_____	laugh	_____
tell	_____	mak	_____
councill	_____	skat	_____
farm	_____	swimm	_____
justifi	_____		

H	J	D	P	U	R	N	W	Z	D	J	E	E	I	S
E	L	B	I	T	S	E	G	G	U	S	L	K	N	K
Q	L	J	L	Z	R	E	K	S	B	B	B	F	S	A
S	H	B	Y	A	L	O	T	A	I	D	A	F	P	T
K	W	F	I	B	U	I	N	S	M	R	E	J	E	E
N	R	I	A	T	F	G	R	R	M	A	C	O	C	R
K	U	V	M	I	R	E	H	E	E	P	I	E	T	O
Q	O	F	A	M	V	E	R	A	E	V	T	G	O	T
L	T	B	N	E	E	V	V	L	B	V	O	Z	R	C
F	L	Z	R	W	Q	R	I	N	H	L	N	G	U	E
E	Q	E	P	O	R	G	F	G	O	Q	E	N	M	R
C	O	U	N	C	I	L	L	O	R	C	B	L	Q	I
A	C	P	O	B	R	O	Y	E	V	R	U	S	L	D
M	O	K	L	E	G	I	B	L	E	S	J	L	O	Z
T	R	E	L	L	E	T	W	S	P	D	M	V	T	F

> 4.11 Finish your story

Focus

1 <u>Underline</u> any spellings in this passage that need correcting
and then write the correctly spelled words above them.

> The problem is that Erth has been obliterated. It meens that you wont
>
> be able to go home ever agen. But don't worrie, the universe is full of
>
> fassinating places. You coud choose to live anywere. Youll sea – you will
>
> hardlie mis it after a wile.

Practice

2 Insert the missing punctuation in this passage.

> Where is your courage snapped Ford Prefect
>
> Its never deserted you before
>
> But look screeched a terrified voice
>
> Thats the Dentrassi exclaimed Ford Id know
>
> that ugly appearance anywhere
>
> Whats that noise

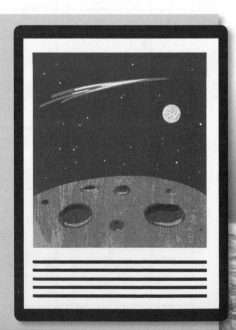

Challenge

3 You can create suspense with *if clauses*. Complete the following sentences.

a If the Vogons had discovered Ford and Arthur, _____

_____

b If Arthur had known that he was about to leave everything he had ever known,

_____

c If the Dentrassi hadn't made such a noise, _____

_____

d If you were to change your mind, _____

_____

e If *The Hitchhiker's Guide to the Galaxy* could explain, _____

_____

4 Complete the following sentences with *if clauses*.

Don't forget to separate the *if clause* from the rest of the sentence with a comma.

a _____ I would not be in this mess.

b _____ will *The Hitchhiker's Guide* tell me?

c _____ the Vogons will eat us for breakfast.

d _____ you will need to hitch a ride to the third star.

e _____ we will get there in no time.

> 4.12 Take part in a Readaloudathon

Focus

> When you review your work, always check it for flow. Using too many short, simple sentences can sound stilted. Check if any of your sentences could join up and whether you have used unnecessary words. **Example:**
>
> The <u>tired</u> travellers collapsed into the cabin. <u>Exhausted, they both</u> breathed a sigh of relief.
>
> The exhausted travellers collapsed into the cabin and breathed a huge sigh of relief.

1   Combine the pairs of sentences to form shorter sentences that mean the same.

   a   The Vogon was enormous. The gigantic creature grabbed at Arthur.

   _____

   _____

   b   Ford and Arthur raced back. They ran as fast as they could.

   _____

   c   Travelling in space is exciting. Not everyone would enjoy space travel though.

   _____

   _____

   d   Arthur was aghast to see the Vogon. He was also scared.

   _____

e The panicked friends gripped on to *The Hitchhiker's Guide*. *The Hitchhiker's Guide* is a useful book.

_____

_____

Practice

> When you read words aloud, they often sound correct but has the writer used the right homophones?

2 <u>Underline</u> any incorrect homophones in this passage.

Arthur decided to give Ford a peace of his mind. 'Of coarse you wood say this is normal but its knot. Nun of the things that have happened are normal. You are sew shore that won of these Vogons won't find us. I don't no how ewe can bee sow confident. As far as I am concerned, we knead to get out of hear in the next our if we don't want to get court. At the moment, we are just a pear of sitting ducks waiting to be maid into mincemeat by sum grate, green, alien beast. Witch door did you say is the whey out?'

Challenge

3 Write out the passage in Activity 2 with all the corrected homophones.

_____

_____

_____

_____

_____

_____

_____

_____

_____

5 ▶ The facts of the matter

> 5.1 Poles apart

Language focus

We use **connectives** to link sentences and paragraphs.
We also use them in the following ways.

- To introduce similar points.

Examples: similarly, in addition, as well as …

- To introduce opposing points.

Examples: but, although, yet, since, alternatively, however, while, whereas, on the other hand …

Some **connectives** work in pairs to link ideas of equal importance.

Examples: both—and   whether—or   not only—but also   neither—nor
               either—or   rather—or

Focus

1   Look at the photos and compare these two places. Use connectives to complete the statements.

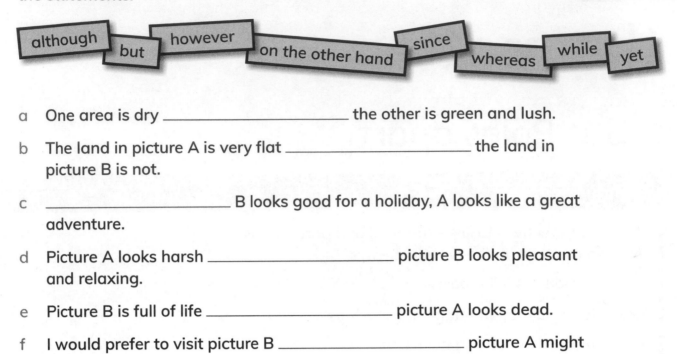

a   One area is dry _____ the other is green and lush.

b   The land in picture A is very flat _____ the land in picture B is not.

c   _____ B looks good for a holiday, A looks like a great adventure.

d   Picture A looks harsh _____ picture B looks pleasant and relaxing.

e   Picture B is full of life _____ picture A looks dead.

f   I would prefer to visit picture B _____ picture A might also be fun.

Practice

2   Use figurative language. Complete these similes to describe picture A in Activity 1. Include your own ideas.

As dry as	As hot as
As hard as	As lifeless as
As cracked as	Like
As parched as	Like

Challenge

3   Write a short paragraph comparing the two places in the photos in Activity 1 or choose any other two places – use your own pictures. Include facts, opinions and figurative language. Use connectives to compare and contrast the information.

_____

_____

_____

_____

> 5.2 A news report

Focus

1   Choose an interesting (child-friendly) news report from an online news web site. Tick (✓) the criteria that apply to it. Add other criteria you think are important.

The report has an interesting headline.	
The first paragraph shows the main idea of the article.	
The report includes mainly facts.	
The report uses different tenses.	
The style and tone of the report is formal and impersonal.	
The language used is correct, standard English.	

2   Analyse your online news report according to purpose, audience, language and layout.

Headline: _____

Purpose: Why was it written?	
Audience: For whom was it written?	
Language: What is the style like? (formal, informal, informative, factual, chatty, direct ...)	
Layout: What does it look like? How is it set out? (colourful, organised, headings, paragraphs, bullets, pictures, graphs ...)	

Practice

3   Write six questions about the article. Begin with Who? What? When? Where?
Why? and How?

_____

_____

_____

_____

_____

_____

Challenge

4   Summarise the information in the news report using a mind map or other suitable form of note taking.

> 5.3 Support a view

Focus

1   Make up a set of five important rules to guide a discussion.

2 Explain the difference between a fact and an opinion.

_____

_____

Practice

3 <u>Underline</u> the facts in each sentence. Rewrite the sentences as facts only.

a   I think it is awful that animal habitats are destroyed by climate change.

_____

b   Are you aware that deforestation is destroying all our forests?

_____

c   It is time that everyone accepts responsibility since climate change affects everyone.

_____

d   It is a shame that animals suffer due to human activity.

_____

e   Some people do not care that the Earth is being destroyed by our careless behaviour.

_____

Challenge

4 For each statement, state why you agree or disagree,
giving points for both sides of the arguments.

Topic	I agree	I disagree
Animals should be kept in zoos for their own protection.		
Cars should be banned in cities.		
Computers could replace teachers.		
Human activity is causing climate change.		

> 5.4 Express possibility

Language focus

A **conditional clause** is a subordinate clause. It expresses the possibility of something that may happen (or might have happened) as a result of something, often using the word **if**.

Example: This area will flood **if** it continues to rain.

A **conditional clause** can go after or before the main clause. If the conditional clause comes first, use a comma to separate it from the main clause.

Example: If it continues to rain, this area will flood.

Focus

1   Give the definition for each of the following.

   a   A simple sentence

   _____

   _____

   b   A compound sentence

   _____

   _____

   c   A complex sentence

   _____

   _____

   d   A main clause

   _____

   _____

e   A subordinate (dependent) clause

_____

_____

Practice

2   Label these sentences as simple, compound or complex.

a   More ice in the polar regions will melt as temperatures rise. _____

b   Climate change affects humans and animals. _____

c   The problem will get worse if we ignore it. _____

d   Climate change is the main problem facing humans. _____

e   Young people need adults and industry to change. _____

3   Change the position of the conditional clause in each sentence and rewrite it using correct punctuation.

a   The match will resume if it stops raining.

_____

b   Unless it rains, you can go out to play.

_____

c   It will be cold when it snows.

_____

d   You can go outside as long as you take an umbrella.

_____

_____

e   Provided you are well, we can go on holiday.

_____

_____

f   They will be warm, if they all take their jackets.

_____

_____

Challenge

4   Complete the following sentences with a main clause.

a   If we ignore the problem of climate change, _____

_____

b   If temperatures continue to rise, _____

_____

c   If animal habitats are destroyed, _____

_____

d   If everyone uses less electricity, _____

_____

e   If we start a climate change campaign, _____

_____

> 5.5 Keep it formal

Language focus

The **active** and **passive voices** are different ways of expressing meaning in a sentence.

In the **active voice**, the subject does the action.

Example: Scientists issued a report.

In the **passive voice**, the agent (or doer) is not the subject.

Example: A report was issued by scientists.

The **active voice** is the most usual in standard English, but the **passive voice** is useful if the agent needs to be hidden or is not important.

Example: A report was issued.

The focus of the sentence is the report not the agent (or doer).

Focus

1   Circle the best words to complete the sentences.

- The active voice is the most (unusual / usual) in standard English.

- A formal report should use (standard / unconventional) English.

- Avoid (formal / informal) language in a formal report.

- The style of a report should be (personal / impersonal).

- Avoid the use of (first- / third-) person pronouns.

- Colloquial expressions and contractions (should / should not) appear in a report.

Practice

2 Rewrite these sentences in an impersonal style.
   Change the pronouns to articles (a, an and the).

   a Hand in your report on climate change.

   _____

   b Our planet is showing signs of human destruction.

   _____

   c My teacher gave her opinion on the issue.

   _____

   d Everyone is responsible for taking care of their environment.

   _____

   e My solution is to use my bicycle.

   _____

3 Complete this table showing how these contractions should be written in a formal text.

I'm = I am	I've =	I'd =
I'll =	we're =	we've =
we'd =	we'll =	they're =
they've =	they'd =	they'll =
haven't =	mustn't =	couldn't =
wouldn't =	can't =	won't =
don't =	would've =	should've =

Challenge

4   Read the sentences. Write A for active or P for passive.
    Then, rewrite each sentence in the other voice.

		A/P
a	Individuals must take responsibility.	
b	The homework on climate change must be completed by everyone.	
c	The learners will conduct a survey.	
d	A plan must be implemented by you.	
e	The council must clean up the area before it becomes a problem.	
f	The report must be completed by the class.	

Writing tip

When you change verbs from the active to passive voice, the passive verbs are formed using the verb to be.

Example: The report **was** finalised yesterday.

To be verbs include be, being, been, am, is, are, was and were.

> 5.6 A balanced report

Focus

1   Read the report and then list five features you notice.

Is it time to ban cars from city centres?

Air pollution is a serious issue and it affects us all directly. Action may be needed to reduce air pollution created by the traffic on our roads.

Over the past few decades, a **significant** increase in the number of cars on the road has resulted in more carbon dioxide **emissions**. Scientists are warning that high levels of CO_2 in the atmosphere cause the Earth to heat up. As a result, we are experiencing more extreme weather patterns. In addition, air pollution in cities causes health problems like asthma. A **ban** on cars in city centres would therefore reduce air pollution and also improve traffic jams and health issues.

On the other hand, such a ban could create other problems. In some cities, public transport is expensive, unreliable or non-existent. In addition, public transport systems would need to be upgraded to cope with greater demand; this requires time and money. Furthermore, personal choice is an issue. For example, some people enjoy using public transport, but others feel safer in their cars than on a bus or a train. Hence, they may object to being forced to use another **mode** of transport.

While there is clearly an urgent need to reduce air pollution, we could achieve this in a number of ways. Rather than banning cars in cities, people could be made aware of the issues and be encouraged to use less fuel and make use of public transport where possible.

Practice

2   Answer the questions to analyse the report in Activity 1.

a   What is the main idea of the report?

_____

b   How many sides are presented in this report?
State each side in one clear sentence.

_____

_____

c   What do the bold words in the report mean? Use a dictionary or thesaurus
if necessary.

- ban   _____

- significant   _____

- emissions   _____

- mode   _____

d   Is this report relevant to you (something that affects you)?
Support your answer with reasons.

_____

_____

_____

e   What is your response to this report? What can <u>you</u> do about it?

_____

_____

_____

> A balanced report
> (or argument) is **objective**. It presents
> all aspects of an issue and then leaves the
> readers to make up their own minds about
> which side of the issue they support.

Challenge

3   Summarise the report as a mind map.

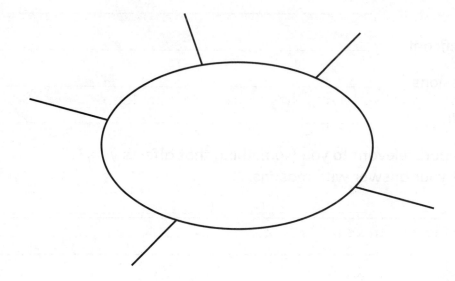

› 5.7 Language techniques

Focus

1   Underline the modal verb in each sentence and circle the correct verb to accompany it.

   a   If you disagree with me, I might (changed / change / changes) your mind.

   b   If the sun shines, we can (drove / drive / driving) to the river.

   c   If we get there early, we could (ate / eat / eaten) our lunch.

   d   If we all stick together, we should (made / make / makes) it back safely.

   e   If you look carefully, you might (found / find / finding) your coins.

   f   If everyone tidied up, we would all (enjoyed / enjoy / enjoys) a neater classroom.

Practice

2   Underline the modal verbs and then complete the sentences using your own words.

   a   We should get there on time if _____

   b   I might be able to help if _____

   c   He may meet us there if _____

   d   You ought to stay here if _____

   e   It would be a perfect day if _____

Challenge

3   Rewrite each sentence adding modal verbs to express possibility.
    Use the connectives in brackets to add clauses to complete the sentences.

a   Animals become extinct. (*if*)

_____

_____

b   Global problems increase daily. (*unless*)

_____

_____

c   Young people have the solution to the problem. (*so*)

_____

_____

d   Leaders make a difference. (*but*)

_____

_____

e   Children lead the way. (*when*)

_____

_____

> 5.8 and 5.9 Present a balanced view

Focus

1 List points for and against the following topic using facts and opinions to support each view.

Learners should cycle to school to help fight climate change.	
For	**Against**

Practice

2 To plan a balanced report on this topic, consider the audience, purpose, language and layout. Complete the table.

Who is this report aimed at?	
What is its purpose and why is it needed?	
What language, style and tone will suit the audience and the purpose?	
How should the report look?	

3   Use a template to plan your balanced report.

Introduction: (Many people believe that … while some think …)		
Viewpoint 1 (Firstly, Finally, As a result …)	**Viewpoint 2** (Despite, However, Therefore …)	**Viewpoint 3 (Optional)** (Similarly … Although …)
Closing statement (So it is clear that on the one hand … while on the other hand …)		

Challenge

4   Write a first draft of the report. Proofread and edit it.

_____

_____

_____

_____

_____

_____

_____

_____

_____

_____

_____

_____

> 5.10 A strong viewpoint

Focus

1 Use a thesaurus to find synonyms and antonyms for the adjective *balanced*.

Synonyms	Antonyms

Practice

2 For each of the following words, choose three synonyms and arrange them from least to most intense on a scale of 1–4. The first is done for you. You will find a thesaurus and a dictionary helpful.

shrink (v)   strike (v)   ally (n)   fight (v)   elegant (adj)

1	2	3	4
lessen	shrink	dwindle	shrivel

Challenge

3   Choose one word and its synonyms from Activity 2.
Write four similar sentences using a different synonym each time.

_____

_____

_____

_____

> 5.11 Pick a side

Focus

1   Carry out a survey to find out how you and other learners in your group feel about different issues. Record responses by ticking (✓) the relevant boxes. Afterwards you can count and compare the responses to see if everyone thinks the same or differently.

Things we must do to make a difference	Strongly agree	Agree	Disagree	Strongly disagree	Not sure
Ban cars in cities					
Stop climate change					
Reduce air pollution					
Eat less meat					
Cut down on using electricity in homes					

Practice

2 Write a complex sentence for each topic, expressing your views. Use these connectives to make your point.

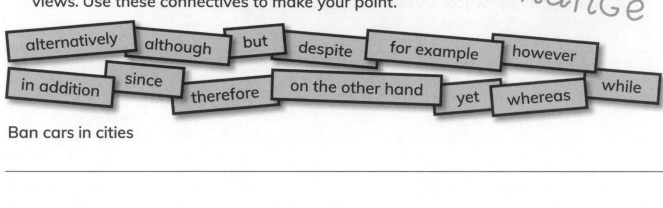

alternatively although but despite for example however
in addition since therefore on the other hand yet whereas while

Ban cars in cities

_____

_____

_____

Stop climate change

_____

_____

_____

Reduce air pollution

_____

_____

_____

Eat less meat

_____

_____

_____

_____

Cut down on using electricity in homes

_____

_____

_____

_____

Challenge

3   Choose one of the topics in Activity 1 and write a persuasive paragraph
    to express your opinion. Use facts and reasons to support your view.
    Include strong vocabulary to sound persuasive.

_____

_____

_____

_____

_____

_____

› 5.12 Have a class debate

Focus

1   In your own words, explain what a debate is.
    Then write five rules for holding a debate.

_____

_____

Practice

2   Read a persuasive speech then answer the questions.

> **Let's curb global warming together**
>
> Global warming is a global issue. This means we are all in it together! Humans have caused the problem and we need to help solve it. Everyone must do their bit to heal our ailing Earth.
>
> The first step is to take stock of how much litter YOU create. Try this experiment: for one week, collect ALL your rubbish in a bag. Multiply that by the number of people in your class – you will be shocked! Clearly – it's time to cut down on waste.
>
> Following this, analyse your rubbish! Are you guilty of throwing away plastic? It is time to cut down on buying plastic goods if all you do is throw them away! Tons of non-degradable plastic is discarded daily, consequently poisoning and cluttering up our environment. Earth is the only home we have – let's look after it.
>
> Last, but not least, we must take 're-using' seriously. Have you started re-using plastic bags, bottles and even drinking straws? It may seem insignificant but imagine if 8 billion people re-used these small items. That's a big deal!
>
> Clearly, we can ALL make a difference – there's NO excuse! As a wise person once said, 'Every little bit helps.' Start today and be part of the global solution.

a   What is the speaker's view on global warming?

_____

_____

b   According to the speaker, what must everyone do?

_____

_____

c Do you agree with this view? What is your view on this matter?
Support your view with facts.

_____

_____

d Identify three connectives used in the speech to make a point.

_____

_____

e Identify three examples of persuasive language in the speech.

_____

_____

_____

Challenge

3 Look at these headlines and consider the other side of the argument about global warming. Then use the template to plan a persuasive speech to support this view.

Latest evidence: Human activity not responsible for climate change

New report dismisses human-caused global warming

Scientists agree – climate change is inevitable!

Arctic melt – not our fault!

Topic:
Introduction:

First point:

Second point:

Third point:

Conclusion:

6 ▶ Poetry at play

6.1 Poetic licence

Focus

1   In your own words, explain the meaning of the term *poetic licence*.

_____

_____

Practice

2   Read the poem *One Day* and then answer the questions.

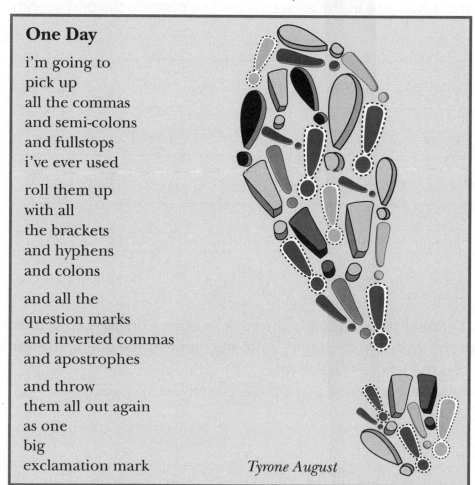

One Day

i'm going to
pick up
all the commas
and semi-colons
and fullstops
i've ever used

roll them up
with all
the brackets
and hyphens
and colons

and all the
question marks
and inverted commas
and apostrophes

and throw
them all out again
as one
big
exclamation mark

Tyrone August

a What punctuation marks are mentioned in the poem *One Day*?

_____

_____

_____

b Does the poem use any punctuation marks? Why?

_____

c Describe the mood of 'the voice' (the speaker).

_____

d Rewrite the poem *One Day*, using correct punctuation and complete sentences. Explain the difference in the effect in how the poem looks and sounds.

_____

_____

_____

_____

Challenge

3 Research other poems and identify the voice in each – an object, an animal, a narrator or the writer. In the table, write the name of the poem, the name of the poet and the voice in the poem.

Name of the poem	Writer	Voice
One Day	Tyrone August	the writer

6.2 A string of words

Language focus

Poets play with words. They use words that are easily confused to create an effect.

Homophones are words that sound the same but have different spellings and meanings.

Examples: write and right, aloud and allowed, past and passed, advice and advise, desert and dessert

Homonyms are words that look and sound alike but have multiple meanings.

Examples: light, bark, nails, jam, pool, mine, bolt, season, novel, current, hatch and racket

Words can mean different things in different cultures.

Examples: trainers, jam or jersey

Focus

1 Read the poem *How do you spell English?* aloud. <u>Underline</u> words you find confusing.

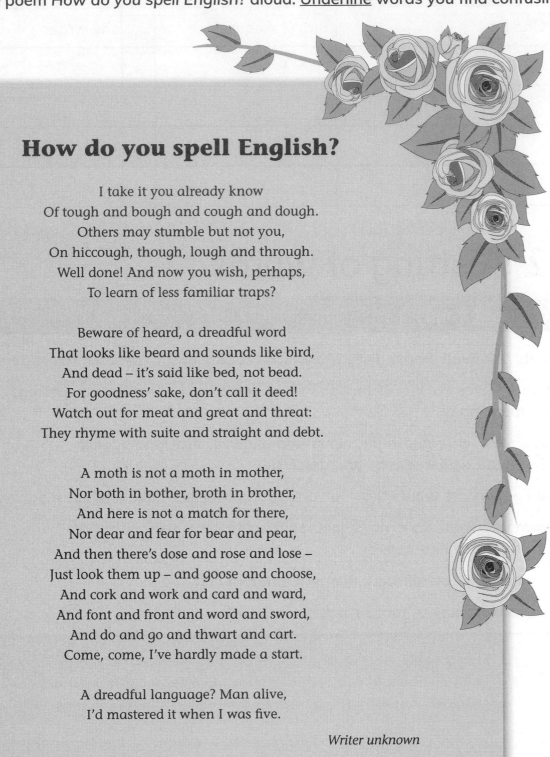

How do you spell English?

I take it you already know
Of tough and bough and cough and dough.
Others may stumble but not you,
On hiccough, though, lough and through.
Well done! And now you wish, perhaps,
To learn of less familiar traps?

Beware of heard, a dreadful word
That looks like beard and sounds like bird,
And dead – it's said like bed, not bead.
For goodness' sake, don't call it deed!
Watch out for meat and great and threat:
They rhyme with suite and straight and debt.

A moth is not a moth in mother,
Nor both in bother, broth in brother,
And here is not a match for there,
Nor dear and fear for bear and pear,
And then there's dose and rose and lose –
Just look them up – and goose and choose,
And cork and work and card and ward,
And font and front and word and sword,
And do and go and thwart and cart.
Come, come, I've hardly made a start.

A dreadful language? Man alive,
I'd mastered it when I was five.

Writer unknown

2 Complete the table with words that have the same sound but a different spelling.
   List words from the poem then add some of your own words to each list.

dead	meat	great	threat	heard
bed				

Practice

3 Find two homophones, or near homophones, for each word.
   Write them in the empty columns in the table.
   Give a short definition or explanatory phrase under each word.

by		
to		
their		
we're		
very		
saw		

Challenge

4   Choose two words from the boxes. For each word, write two sentences to show the different meanings. Use a dictionary to help you.

bark   bolt   current   hatch   jam   light
mine   nails   novel   pool   racket   season

_____

_____

_____

_____

6.3 Patterns and shapes

Focus

1   Compare two forms of cinquain. Describe the features of each.

Ⓐ **Going fishing**	Ⓑ **Let's go fishing**
Fishing Silent, patient … Watching, waiting, wondering I'm getting really bored Swim-time!	Fishing I cast off and Eagerly watch and wait. After ten minutes I am bored. Let's swim!

Practice

2 Revise word classes.
Find a related word for each word class and write them in the table.

Nouns (common and abstract)	Adjectives (comparative and superlative)	Verbs	Adverbs
creation			
			imaginatively
	attractive		
		obey	
love			
			softly
		succeed	
	breathless		

Challenge

3 Find synonyms with different syllable counts.
   Fill in the table with as many synonyms as possible.

One syllable	Two syllables	Three syllables	Four or more syllables
new			
			nevertheless
	perish		
		gingerly	
light			
	wriggle		
		sovereign	

6.4 Follow the rules

Focus

1 Plan a cinquain poem.

   • Choose which type of cinquain poem you will write – word count or syllable count.

   • Choose a topic.

   • Use this space to brainstorm words, phrases, images, ideas, synonyms and different word classes.

Practice

2   Write your cinquain, and then check and edit it.
    Show your corrections and improvements.

_____

_____

_____

_____

Challenge

3   Rewrite your cinquain neatly and illustrate it.

6.5 Laugh with limericks

Language focus

A **limerick** is a five-line humorous verse with a characteristic pattern of syllables and **rhythm**. The DUM words carry the beat or clap.

Lines 1, 2 and 5 have between seven and nine syllables and three beats.
Clap: da DUM da da DUM da da DUM

Lines 3 and 4 have between five and seven syllables and two beats.
Clap: da DUM da da DUM

A **limerick** also has a strict **rhyme scheme:** AABBA.

A **limerick** is a nonsense verse, which means it might not always make sense.

Limericks may use figurative language to create an image and make the reader laugh.

Focus

1   Pair the rhyming words in the word box and then find them in the word search. Circle each rhyming pair in a different colour in the word search.

Look out for other rhyming word pairs in the word search.

> agree away dough fair flower heart hour know lime
> nought part pie puff rare rough saw sea should
> six sore sort steer sticks thyme true wood

N	R	Q	E	H	W	Z	W	N	T	Z	I	T	Z	B
H	T	X	Z	U	G	E	S	Q	M	M	A	H	I	F
F	L	O	W	E	R	U	I	I	C	D	S	Y	H	L
I	G	M	P	X	T	T	O	R	X	W	K	M	H	N
I	N	U	E	A	E	R	Y	D	T	H	C	E	G	S
H	F	P	G	R	A	I	O	V	Z	E	I	X	U	M
F	D	R	A	A	F	E	J	S	N	Y	T	O	O	Y
I	E	R	W	T	H	E	W	E	D	O	S	Q	R	I
E	A	A	R	D	X	O	R	L	O	X	U	R	V	R
I	Y	A	F	O	Z	P	U	F	A	I	R	G	Z	Y
H	E	E	Q	O	A	O	T	R	J	Q	N	W	H	E
H	G	S	G	W	H	K	E	R	O	S	A	G	K	T
L	I	M	E	S	N	N	Q	P	Q	S	Y	P	G	L
R	E	E	T	S	Q	O	T	R	A	P	I	Q	T	V
X	Z	B	P	R	P	W	B	T	F	E	D	B	B	N

Practice

2 Read a limerick by the famous poet Edward Lear. Show the rhythm in the limerick by <u>underlining</u> the words or parts of words that carry the beat.

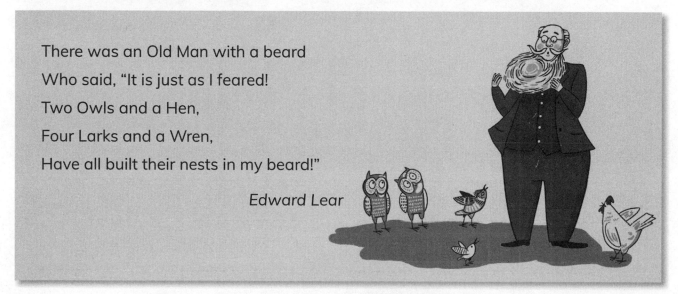

There was an Old Man with a beard

Who said, "It is just as I feared!

Two Owls and a Hen,

Four Larks and a Wren,

Have all built their nests in my beard!"

Edward Lear

Challenge

3   Research limericks. Find out five facts about limericks including
    when they began and who made them popular.

    _____

    _____

    _____

    _____

    _____

6.6 Play with words

Focus, Practice and Challenge

Have some fun writing your own limericks. Use this space to plan and check your work.
Choose your favourite limericks to write out and display in the classroom.

7 > A different medium

> 7.1 A multimedia novel

Focus

Using precise verbs

1 Choose a powerful verb to replace the underlined words.

Example: Miriam <u>walked slowly</u> down the path. _____ dawdled _____

a Annika dropped a glass and it <u>broke completely</u>. _____

b The teacher <u>looked quickly</u> at the homework tasks. _____

c Hendrik <u>carefully hid</u> the box under his bed. _____

d Marcia <u>looked crossly</u> at her brother. _____

e The cat <u>walked unevenly</u> across the town square. _____

Practice

2 Make a word web of ten more vivid verbs to replace went.

went is the past tense form of the verb *go* – make sure your verbs are also in the past tense.

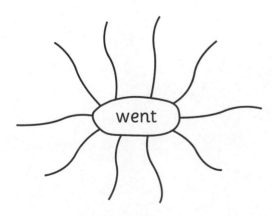

went

Challenge

3   Choose a more interesting word to replace each of the <u>underlined</u> words.

Flora <u>saw</u> _____ Mrs Tickham in the garden being <u>pulled</u>

_____ around by her <u>new</u> _____ vacuum

cleaner. Then she saw the <u>powerful</u> _____ vacuum cleaner

<u>suck up</u> _____ a <u>small</u>

_____ squirrel. Flora

<u>let out a cry</u> _____. She

<u>went</u> _____ up, <u>took</u>

_____ the machine

and <u>pulled</u> _____

out the plug. She <u>looked carefully</u>

_____ inside and was

able to <u>get</u> _____

the <u>frightened</u> _____

squirrel by opening up the vacuum

cleaner. The squirrel <u>looked up</u>

_____ at her with

steady eyes. Flora could almost believe

the squirrel was thanking her.

> 7.2 Language matters

> **Language focus**
>
> **A new paragraph** usually signals a change of action, time, place, idea or speaker. Sometimes a new paragraph is used to emphasise an idea or a few important words.
>
> **A compound sentence** is formed when you join two related main clauses with a connective.
>
> **Example connectives:** for, and, nor, but, or, yet, so
>
> **Example sentence:** The sun was shining <u>but</u> then it rained.
>
> **A complex sentence** contains a main clause and one or more dependent clauses, usually linked by a connective.
>
> **Example connectives:** if, although, unless, because, after, since, when
>
> **Example sentence:** They were tired <u>because</u> they had been on a long walk.

Focus

Compound sentences

1 <u>Underline</u> the connectives in these compound sentences.

   a Flora felt a little guilty but continued reading her comic.

   b Stop reading that comic or you will break the contract.

   c Flora's mother wanted to try the new vacuum cleaner so she pressed the ON button.

   d The squirrel was gobbled up by the vacuum cleaner yet it remained unharmed.

   e Flora was pleased the squirrel was fine for she hated to think it could have been hurt.

Practice

Compound or complex sentences

2 Underline the connectives and identify the sentences as compound or complex.

a The floor will stay clean unless you forget to take off your muddy boots.

   _____

b I want to read my comic so I will have to break the contract. _____

c Flora admitted she had been reading her comic because she did not

   want to lie. _____

d I want to rescue the squirrel but I don't know how to do it. _____

e When you turn on the vacuum cleaner, hold on to it tightly. _____

Challenge

Paragraphs

3 Write down five reasons to start a new paragraph.

   _____

   _____

   _____

   _____

   _____

4 Identify whether each sentence is simple, compound or complex.

> [a] Flora discovered something unusual about the squirrel. [b] The squirrel's name was Ulysses and he could fly. [c] Flora decided to keep this a secret because she did not want her mother to make a fuss. [d] Later that night, she found Ulysses at the typewriter, so she went over to him. [e] She read his typing since it seemed to make sense. [f] It was a poem.

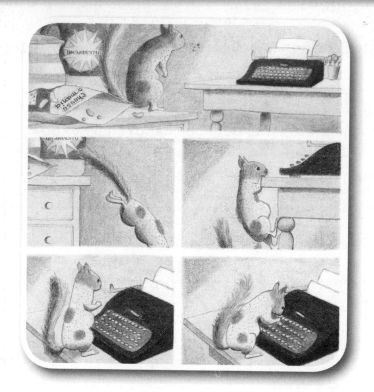

a _____

b _____

c _____

d _____

e _____

f _____

> 7.3 and 7.4 Plan and write an illustrated episode

Focus

1 Fill in this table to plan the first chapter of a multimedia adventure story.

	Ideas for the chapter paragraphs	Multimedia features
Introduction Set scene and grab attention		Cartoon sequence to set scene
Build-up to problem or complication		Illustrations
Problem or complication climax		
Resolution – lead-in to next chapter		Ellipsis

Practice

2 Write a cartoon sequence to begin your chapter. Include short narrative as well as dialogue.

<table>
<tr><td></td><td></td></tr>
<tr><td></td><td></td></tr>
</table>

Challenge

3 Write the introductory paragraphs to the chapter following on from the cartoon sequence. Bring the characters to life with interesting or quirky details – what they look like, what they are doing, what they are thinking and what they say.

_____

_____

_____

_____

_____

_____

_____

_____

_____

_____

_____

_____

_____

_____

_____

_____

_____

_____

_____

> 7.5 Introducing manga

Focus

1   Study the picture carefully and list the features on the front cover. Explain what each one is for.

Example: Illustrator's name – to identify who did the artwork.

- _____
  _____

- _____
  _____

- _____
  _____

- _____
  _____

Ever since Itsuki found a box washed up on the beach, everything has been different. He could not rest until he found a way to open it. Little did he know that it was no ordinary box …

"A great read. Action packed time travel adventure!"

Itsuki's Surprise

Sato Yumi

ITSUKI'S SURPRISE
Volume 2

Story by
Sato Yumi

Art by
KENZO

Contents
Prologue   1
Chapter 1   3
Chapter 2   27
Chapter 3   65
Chapter 4   91

Practice

2   List the features on the back cover, spine and contents page and explain what each one is for.

- _____
- _____
- _____
- _____
- _____
- _____
- _____
- _____

Challenge

3 Notice the detail.

   a What is the effect of the question mark and exclamation marks on the front cover?

   _____

   b Explain how you would read the book based on the layout of the cover.

   _____

   c What is the effect of the ellipsis at the end of the blurb?

   _____

   d What sort of adventure is the book about?

   _____

   _____

   e How do you think the adventure starts?

   _____

   _____

   f How long is the prologue?

   _____

   g What do you think happens in the prologue?

   _____

   _____

   _____

   h Would you enjoy reading this story? Give your reasons.

   _____

   _____

   _____

> 7.6 Shion

Focus

1 Create an imaginary character profile of Itsuki on a mind map.
Use the book cover in Session 7.5 Activity 1 as well as
your imagination.

dark haired boy aged about 11

Practice

2 Write up your character profile in a paragraph.
Remember to start with a topic sentence and use a variety of sentence types.

_____

_____

_____

_____

_____

_____

_____

_____

_____

Challenge

3 Write an outline of events that you think might be contained in each of the book's chapters. Remember to think about story structure and the genre. Give each chapter a title as well.

Prologue	
Chapter 1 _____	
Chapter 2 _____	
Chapter 3 _____	
Chapter 4 _____	

> 7.7 Medium matters

Focus

1   Rewrite the story in this cartoon in standard narrative format.

    a   Use all the information to develop the narrative content in your own words.

    b   Punctuate any dialogue correctly.

_____

_____

_____

_____

_____

_____

_____

Practice

2   Edit and improve your writing.

    a   Use a thesaurus and a dictionary to check your spelling and to find more interesting words to use.

    b   Think about text effects that you could use to add to the narrative.

Challenge

3   Choose a book you have read or know well. Complete the form to help decide whether you would enjoy it more or less in graphic novel or comic book format.

My chosen book:

Author:

Publisher: Genre:

Features of book: (*chapters, illustrations, prologue, flashback, etc.*)

Plot summary:

Main characters:

What would work well in graphic novel format:

What would be difficult in graphic novel format:

Which format I prefer to read and why:

> 7.8 All the world's a stage

Focus

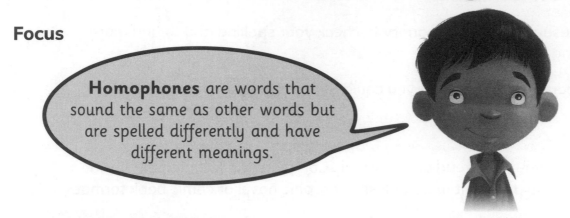

Homophones are words that sound the same as other words but are spelled differently and have different meanings.

1   Identify the homophones.

a   In this passage ten incorrect homophones are <u>underlined</u>.
Copy them into the table and then write the correct homophones next to them to make sense of the passage. The first one has been done for you.

> Shakespeare was a famous poet as well as a [a] <u>playwrite</u>. We [b] <u>no</u> he [c] <u>rote</u> 154 sonnets. A sonnet is a poem of 14 lines with a special rhyme scheme. [d] <u>Their</u> are several types of sonnets but Shakespeare always followed the rhyming pattern ABABCDCDEFEFGG. Each group of [e] <u>for</u> lines is called a quatrain and the final [f] <u>too</u> lines are called a rhyming couplet – can you [g] <u>sea</u> why? Each line has ten syllables – five [h] <u>pears</u> of syllables ([i] <u>witch</u> are called [j] <u>feat</u>) giving the rhythm deDUM-deDUM-deDUM-deDUM-deDUM.

Incorrect	Correct		Incorrect	Correct
a playwrite	playwright		f	
b			g	
c			h	
d			i	
e			j	

Practice

Collective nouns name groups of things like people, objects or animals. Although the group is made up of more than one thing, the collective noun usually takes a singular verb: Shakespeare's <u>troupe of actors was</u> one of the most famous in the world.

2 Circle the correct verb forms to match the collective nouns.

Example: My anthology of poems (are / (is)) one of my family's favourite books.

a A flock of birds (have / has) just taken off to migrate.

b I hope the audience (enjoy / enjoys) the show.

c A shoal of fish (were / was) darting through the water.

d A group of islands (are / is) called an archipelago.

e At sunset, the same pride of lions always (appear / appears) at the waterhole.

Challenge

3 Read the extract.

a Rewrite it as a play script with stage directions.

b Invent and write the rest of Viola's reply to the Captain.

Extract based on *Twelfth Night*

"Who is Olivia?" asked Viola looking thoughtful.

"She is the daughter of a count," replied the Captain. "The count died and left her to be looked after by her brother. But would you know it – he also died shortly after …" The Captain shook his head as he thought of Olivia's troubles.

"What a sad thing!" exclaimed Viola. "Does she favour the Duke Orsino's suit?"

"No one knows my good lady," continued the Captain, "for she will see no man admitted to her house so much is she grieving the death of her poor brother."

"Well," said Viola, folding her arms, …"

Adaptation of *Twelfth Night* by William Shakespeare

Act I Scene II

Viola and the Captain are …

_____ : _____

_____ : _____

_____

_____

_____

_____

_____

_____ : _____

_____ : _____

_____

_____

_____

_____ : _____

_____

_____

_____

> 7.9 What has changed?

Focus

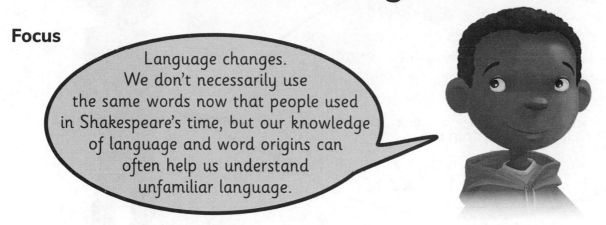

Language changes.
We don't necessarily use
the same words now that people used
in Shakespeare's time, but our knowledge
of language and word origins can
often help us understand
unfamiliar language.

1   Each crossword clue is an old-fashioned contraction.
Write the full word or words into the crossword space.

Across

4   'tisn't

8   e'er

9   shan't

10   'tween

11   'twas

Down

1   mayn't

2   'tis

3   'twasn't

5   o'er

6   crush'd

7   ne'er

Practice

Shakespeare is said to have added over 2000 words and phrases to the English language. Some are still in use today like *fashionable, cold-blooded, new-fangled, scuffle* and *swagger*. However, some words common in Shakespeare's day are no longer in common use; for example, *thou* is an old-fashioned form of *you* and *art* is an older form of *are – How art thou today?*

2 Try your hand at writing in Shakespearean language.

a Look at the words in each column of the table. Use your prior knowledge and experience to identify the word classes and complete the column headings.

_____	_____	_____
fawning	boil-brained	dewberry
loggerheaded	rough-hewn	gudgeon
mewling	idle-headed	clotpole
saucy	spleeny-brained	measle
churlish	motley-minded	barnacle
craven	clay-brained	miscreant
mammering	clapper-clawed	giglet
spleeny	dismal-dreaming	fustilarian
pribbling	hasty-witted	minnow
dissembling	knotty-pated	baggage
droning	onion-eyed	mammet

b Shakespeare's plays are full of arguments and banter between characters. Have fun inventing your own Shakespearean expressions.

- Choose one word from each column and begin each expression with *Thou*. Aim for some alliteration.

- Practise saying each expression aloud with appropriate feeling and tone. It does not matter what it means – it is the sound that counts.

Example: Thou mewling, motley-minded miscreant!

Thou _____!

Thou _____!

Thou _____!

Thou _____!

Thou _____!

Challenge

3   Consider the detail.

a   Why do you think each expression in Activity 2b has an exclamation mark at the end?

_____

b   Re-read the words in the middle column in Activity 2a.

- Explain why they all have a hyphen.

_____

- Write down at least five modern words created in the same way.

_____

_____

c   Write a more modern version of two of the exclamations you wrote in Activity 2b. Include the same types of words: adjectives, compound adjectives and nouns.

You _____!

You _____!

> 7.10 Using language

Focus

Language focus

A **semicolon** creates variety by joining short sentences. It creates a break. The break is more than a comma but less than a full stop.

A **semicolon** can join two closely related main clauses without a connective.

Example: Bring your reading book tomorrow; you will need it in first period.

It is used before a connective (**examples:** however, therefore, for example, finally, on the other hand) when it introduces a complete sentence.

Example: You will need to bring some money; however, don't bring too much.

It separates list items where a comma might cause confusion.

Example: The school has learners from Paris, France; Tehran, Iran; and Lima, Peru.

---

1   Use semicolons. Read each sentence carefully and decide where to place the semicolon.

   Example: Abdul likes to play chess; Idris prefers to read.

   a   The hall was silent only the distant whispering behind scenes could be heard.

   b   The play was a great success all the actors remembered their lines perfectly.

   c   In summer it is warm and dry in winter it is cold and wet.

   d   The athletes were exhausted it was a long, gruelling race.

   e   Lindiwe's mother is a lawyer my mother is a doctor.

Practice

2   Add the commas and semicolons to this list.

> The winners of the local art competition were Jo Ackerman Rusternberg Junior School Vuyiswa Doo Bergvliet Primary School Willem van Biljon Greenway Junior School and Rose Makwenda Timour Hall Primary School.

Challenge

Language focus

A **colon** introduces any of these: a speaker, dialogue, a list, an idea or an explanation.

Examples: We have many gadgets: televisions, tablets, laptops and smart phones.
We have cancelled tonight's production: the lead actor is sick.

A **colon** is especially useful for adding emphasis to part of a sentence.

Example: I enjoy one subject the most: English.

3   Add colons to the sentences.

Example: Wiremu announced: 'I want to be a rugby player like my dad.'

a   This is what will be in your geography test continents, oceans, seas, the equator, the tropics of Capricorn and Cancer, and capital cities.

b   I can't believe where we are going on holiday Hawaii!

c   The principal said 'Please sit down.'

d   Ingredients tomatoes, lettuce leaves, cucumber, radishes and spring onions.

e   **Mother** Remember not to open the window in this storm.

   Shion I wish I could open the window just a little bit …

> 7.11 Shakespeare alive

Focus

1   Label each piece of text on the cartoon with *narrative*, *thoughts*, *dialogue*, *sound effects* or *other* (explain).

narrative Last year...

Read next week's instalments to find out what Atticus has seen.

Practice

2   Write out the cartoon sequence as a play script with stage directions. Invent the names of any characters that don't have one.

Remember to use Roman numerals for the Act and Scene numbers you choose.

Act _____ Scene _____

Challenge

3   Write the next instalment in the story as a cartoon sequence.

- Use text effects and punctuation to add expression.

- Use different-shaped bubbles to indicate speaking, thinking, narrative and sound effects.

- Include brief narrative.

- Use as many boxes as you need to tell the story instalment.

A few minutes later ...

> 7.12 Write your own play script

Focus

1   Write two more instalments to the Atticus story in Session 7.11 as a play script. Plan the two instalments in a storyboard.

> You can use the instalment you wrote in Session 7.11 Activity 3 as your first one.

Scene:	Scene:
Characters:	Characters:
Plot:	Plot:

Practice

2 Set out your play script as two scenes. On the play script, write the title, act and scene numbers as well as information to set the scene, including which characters enter.

Example: Enter Atticus and …

MY PLAY: _____

Act _____ Scene _____

Directions:

_____

_____

_____

_____	_____
_____	_____
_____	_____
_____	_____
_____	_____
_____	_____
_____	_____
_____	_____
_____	_____
_____	_____

Act _____ Scene _____

Directions:

_____

_____

_____

_____	_____
_____	_____
_____	_____
_____	_____
_____	_____
_____	_____
_____	_____
_____	_____
_____	_____
_____	_____
_____	_____
_____	_____
_____	_____
_____	_____

Challenge

3   Write in the dialogue and any other stage directions on your play script in Activity 2. Add your production notes below.

Remember, there is no narrative in a play script. The dialogue has to tell the whole story.

Act out your play with a partner or in a small group.

Production notes

_____

_____

_____

_____

_____

_____

_____

_____

_____

_____

8 Make it happen

> 8.1 Weigh up waste

Focus

1 Try one of these activities to get you thinking about your waste. Record your findings in this box.

- Conduct interviews with learners and teachers. Find out what people do with their rubbish.

- Carry out a survey to find out if anything is needed to help people to recycle.

- Keep a 'waste journal' for a week. Each day record your observations to show how much waste and what waste is generated.

Practice

2   Choose the correct prefix for each word. Write them out.

    a   *dis–* or *mis–*:   please   take   understand

    b   *non–* or *un–*:   grateful   toxic   clean

    c   *un–* or *in–*:   reliable   important   expensive

    d   *im–* or *il–*:   patient   legal   possible

    e   *dis–* or *de–*:   use   compose   part

a   _____   _____   _____

b   _____   _____   _____

c   _____   _____   _____

d   _____   _____   _____

e   _____   _____   _____

Challenge

3   These words can be written with and without a hyphen.
    Use a dictionary to explain the difference in meanings.

    a   recount   _____

        re-count   _____

    b   repress   _____

        re-press   _____

c   recover   _____

     re-cover   _____

d   refuse   _____

     re-fuse   _____

e   resort   _____

     re-sort   _____

Remember to use a **hyphen** before a vowel in words like *re-elect*, *anti-aircraft* and *pro-active*. The prefixes *ex–* and *self–* are usually followed by a hyphen.

> 8.2 An article to startle

Focus

1   Read the magazine article and explore the context and content.

THE SOLE OF THE MATTER

Bethlehem Alemu, founder and managing director of soleRebels Footwear, is making a difference by creating jobs and hope out of old car tyres!

In 2004, Bethlehem Tilahun Alemu left her ordinary accountancy job and started making shoes! Today, her company soleRebels is Africa's largest footwear brand, with her shoes selling in over 50 countries worldwide.

Alemu is one of Africa's most celebrated businesswomen. She has featured on the front cover of many magazines and was selected as a 'Young Global Leader' by the World Economic Forum 2011. She has even won the award for 'Most Outstanding Businesswoman' at the annual African Business Awards.

You may be wondering about the secret to her success. Well, it's no secret! Her enthusiasm is **contagious** as she describes how her success is based on creating jobs by making use of local skills, natural resources and business opportunities. Bethlehem describes how she came up with her brainchild.

'Having grown up in a small village (near Addis Ababa), watching our family and neighbours struggling, we decided to create the "better life" we were all waiting for by harnessing our community's incredible **artisan** skills and channelling them into a **sustainable**, global, fair trade footwear business.'

SoleRebels footwear includes sandals, flip flops and shoes with soles made from recycled car tyres. Her designs use recycled and sustainable materials with hand-spun organic cotton fabrics, and natural fibres including pure Abyssinian **koba**!

'We took this wonderful indigenous age-old recycling tradition and fused it with fantastic Ethiopian artisan crafts and excellent modern design and turned it into footwear that has universal flavour and appeal.'

You are sure to catch a sparkle in her eye as she concludes 'Our motto at soleRebels is: "Making the world a better place, one step at a time". So have fun, help others and be proud that you are making the world a better place. What more could you ask from your shoes …'

Glossary

contagious: infectious

artisan: a skilled, manual worker

sustainable: something that keeps going and maintains itself

koba: an plant that is indigenous to Ethiopia

a   Who is Bethlehem Alemu?

_____

b   What did she decide to do with old car tyres?

_____

c   Where and when did she start a company?

_____

d   Why did she win awards?

_____

e   How does she aim to create jobs?

_____

f   How would you describe her?

_____

Practice

2   Identify the purpose, audience, language and format of the text in Activity 1.
Complete the table and then answer the questions.

a

Purpose	Why was this text written?	
Audience	Who was it written for?	
Language	What is the style like?	
Format	What does it look like? Describe the layout.	

b   Does the article sound factual or persuasive or both? Find examples.

_____

_____

c   How is it organised? Describe the impact of these organisational features.

_____

_____

d   What impact does the heading have on the reader?

_____

_____

e   On a scale of 0–10, how do you think this article rates in level of persuasion?
Explain your choice.

not at all persuasive   **persuasive**   **extremely persuasive**

0 ←   → 10

Challenge

3 Note the similarities and differences between a news report and a magazine article. Use key words and phrases to make notes. Begin with the features in the boxes and add others.

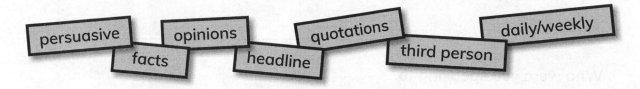

persuasive · opinions · quotations · daily/weekly · facts · headline · third person

Similarities	Differences

> 8.3 Language and features

Focus

1 Fill in the relative pronoun in each sentence. Underline the noun it relates to.

a _____ is the bicycle I would like to buy.

b This is the teacher with _____ you must go.

c These are the volunteers _____ want to help us.

d The two girls, _____ names were on the list, did not arrive.

e Is this the question _____ you do not understand?

Practice

2 Turn the sentences round to change who to whom.
Hint: Begin each sentence with To or From.

a Who would you like the flowers delivered to?

_____

b Who were you speaking to?

_____

c Who did the parcel come from?

_____

d Who did you send the letter to?

_____

e Who does the honour go to?

_____

Challenge

3 Research the rules to explain when to use who or whom and when to use which or that.

a	When to use who or whom	
b	When to use which or that	

› 8.4 Punctuation with purpose

Focus

1 Name the punctuation marks in the table.

,		...	
( )		!	
–		?	
:		' '	

Practice

2 Decide if the following statements about commas are true or false.
If the statement is false, correct it, and if it is true, give an example.

The purpose of a comma is to ...

a separate words in a list. TRUE / FALSE

_____

b separate connectives from the other words in a sentence. TRUE / FALSE

_____

c provide additional essential or non-essential information. TRUE / FALSE

_____

d separate phrases and/or clauses in a sentence. TRUE / FALSE

_____

3 Decide where the comma should go in these sentences.
   Use a coloured pen to fill them in.

a The teacher wants Inam Neo Bekkie Jo and Di to present their
   speeches next week.

b To fill in the form you should print neatly using a black pen without
   making any mistakes.

c You can have extra time to finish however it must be done by tomorrow.

d The book was exciting interesting fun and easy to read.

e Since I'd also like to see the film maybe we should go to see it together.

Challenge

4 Rewrite the sentences using correct punctuation to show clarity.

a The class all voted yes to going home early.

   _____

b She replied I'd love some more.

   _____

c This ice cream has delicious out of this world flavours.

   _____

d He received the title of Best Young Recycler of the year.

   _____

e I think we you and I should redo this work.

   _____

f I can join you if you like for the clean-up.

   _____

5   Write three sentences of your own, using three different ways to show parenthesis (brackets).

_____

_____

_____

> 8.5 Follow instructions

Focus

1   <u>Underline</u> the command verbs in this set of instructions.

How to make papier mâché pulp

What you need: old newspaper, water, flour, large bowl

What to do:

1   Tear up old newspaper into small pieces.

2   Put the pieces into a large bowl.

3   Add enough warm water to cover the paper completely.

4   Leave it to soak for a few hours until it is soft.

5   Mix it up with your hands until smooth.

6   Squeeze out the excess water.

7   Add flour to make a gluey paste.

8   Store it in an air-tight container.

Practice

2 Put these nouns under the correct headings in
the table and then add your own words to each list.

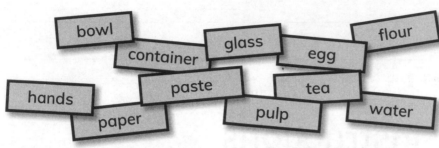

a Countable nouns	b Uncountable nouns	c Both

Challenge

3   Use words from the table in Activity 2 to write short sentences with the quantifiers *less* and *fewer*. Remember: *less* and *fewer* mean the same thing but we generally use *less* for singular (uncountable) nouns and *fewer* for plural (countable) nouns.

Use *less* for singular (uncountable) nouns	Use *fewer* for plural (countable) nouns
Add less <u>flour</u> to make the pulp thicker.	You can add fewer <u>spoons</u> of flour if you like.

> ## 8.6 Clauses to clarify

Language focus

Subordinating **connectives** are used in complex sentences to sequence events and give clarity, especially if two or more things are happening at once.

Examples: **When** the bottle is dry, twist the waste plastic **in order to** get it into the bottle.
Keep the bottle handy **so** it is always there **when** you need it.

Focus

1 Re-order these instructions to make a planting pot, using the connectives as a guide.

You need a plastic 2L bottle.	
To begin, lie the bottle on its side.	
How to make a planting pot	
and poke holes in the 'bottom' side.	
Cut a 10 cm opening in the 'top' side,	
Use the opening to fill it with soil.	
If you water daily, your seeds will grow.	
Finally, plant seeds and water the soil.	

Practice

2   To help you make papier mâché (in Session 8.5), complete the sentences using clauses and phrases from the boxes.

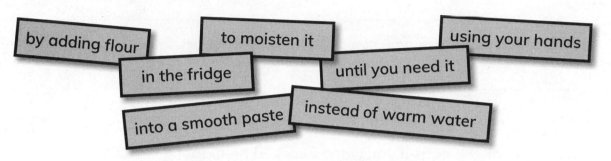

by adding flour   to moisten it   using your hands
in the fridge   until you need it
into a smooth paste   instead of warm water

a   Once the paper has soaked for a few hours, mash it up _____ .

_____ .

b   If you would rather not get your hands dirty, use a blender to mix the pulp

_____ .

c   If you do not want to wait too long, use hot water _____ .

_____ .

d   If it is necessary, add more water _____ .

e   When the pulp is smooth, make a gluey paste _____ .

_____ .

f   In order to make it last, store it in an air-tight container _____ .

_____ .

3   Practise using the *if* clause.
    Rearrange the sentences so the position of the *if* clause changes.

a   If you need to boil water, ask an adult to help you.

_____

b You will need all the ingredients if you want to bake a cake.

_____

_____

c If you finish your work, you can continue with your art.

_____

_____

d You must boil the eggs if you want a cooked breakfast.

_____

_____

e If you make a mess, you must clean up.

_____

_____

Challenge

4 Write five complex sentences using **more than one** subordinating connective from the boxes.

as long as	as ... while	before	even if	in order to	once

providing	so that	therefore	until	when	whenever	yet

Example: Add more water **when** the mixture thickens **in order to** keep it moist.

a _____

b _____

c _____

d _____

e _____

> 8.7 Make something

Focus

1 a Carry out some independent research. Find out how to make
and build things with waste materials. Here are some ideas:

- A model house
- A stationery holder
- A toy car or bicycle
- A door stop

b What else could you make with ordinary waste materials?

_____

_____

_____

_____

Practice

2 Use the template to write a set of instructions for making one of the ideas
in Activity 1 or your own idea. Remember to use command verbs, connectives
and *if* clauses, and keep sentences short and clear.

Topic:		
List of materials:		Picture of final product:
Step 1:	Step 2:	Step 3:

Step 4:	Step 5:	Step 6:

Challenge

3   Change the format of your instructions in Activity 2 to a paragraph.

_____

_____

_____

_____

_____

_____

> 8.8 Demonstrate

Focus

1   List three things that you should **not do** when giving a demonstration on how to make or do something.

_____

_____

_____

_____

Practice

2   Decide which presentation tips are good (✓) and which are not so good (✗).

- Your voice must be very loud. ☐

- Your voice must be clear with a varied tone. ☐

- Keep your eyes open all the time. ☐

- Maintain good eye contact with the audience. ☐

- Always stand still. ☐

- Use body language effectively. ☐

- Make sure the audience pays attention. ☐

- Keep the audience interested with clear, direct instructions. ☐

- Visual props are essential to improve any speech. ☐

- Use visual props to support your speech and add impact if necessary. ☐

Challenge

3   Design an assessment table with a rating system to guide and assess a demonstration on how to make or do something. Use it when you prepare and present or when you listen to someone else's presentation.

> 8.9 Facts and opinions about recycling

Focus

1   Read the text and explore the language and vocabulary. Then answer the questions.

Recycling

Recycling means collecting discarded waste and using it to create a different product. Old items can be recycled in different ways. For example, old tyres can be re-used whole as road barriers or swings for children, or they can be melted down and the rubber used to make new things such as building materials, tiles and sports surfaces.

Years ago, before the invention of plastics and other non-biodegradable materials, disposing of waste was less of a concern. Now that people produce so much non-biodegradable waste, it is more difficult to find places to store it. Much waste is dumped in landfill sites. However, landfill sites take up large areas of land and the waste may remain there for many years – perhaps even centuries – and can pollute the environment. Recycling is an alternative way of dealing with it, reducing the amount of waste in the environment and protecting the planet from pollution. Recycling is also important in the effort to reduce the amount of new materials used for manufacturing things. This is necessary because there is not an unlimited supply of natural resources and they may run out. Furthermore, it can also be more cost-effective to re-use old materials instead of using new ones.

To be a responsible recycler, always check to see whether a product is recycled or can be recycled by looking for the 'recycling loop'.

The three steps in the recycling process are known as 'the three Rs':

- Reduce – Get into the habit of throwing away fewer items and only buy things that you really need, that last a long time or that come with minimal packaging, such as loose fresh produce.

- Re-use – Choose products that can be used again (e.g. rechargeable batteries), mend broken products or find new ways to use things. An old container can become a flower pot, for example.

- Recycle – Use separate bins to collect and separate different types of waste items and take them to a recycling centre. Remember that some items cannot be recycled so it is important to find out how to dispose of them properly. You cannot recycle some oil-based liquid cleaners, for example; allow these liquids to solidify before throwing them out or give some to a friend to use.

a   Identify two words with different prefixes.

_____

b   Identify two words with different suffixes.

_____

c   Identify two hyphenated compound adjectives.

_____

d   Identify two examples of connectives used at the start of a sentence.

_____

Practice

2   Identify the facts and add some opinions about the topic.

Facts	Opinions

Challenge

3   Consider a different viewpoint. Explain why some people find recycling difficult or impossible.

Recycling is difficult because ...

_____

_____

_____

_____

_____

> 8.10 Summarise

Focus

1   <u>Underline</u> the key words and phrases in each sentence.
Focus on important nouns, verbs and adjectives.

  a   Recycling is something we can all do to help save our environment from further damage.

  b   It is important that everyone becomes more aware of how to reduce, re-use and recycle their waste.

  c   It is a challenge to try to re-use any plastic you bring into your home or your workspace.

  d   Every small act can make a big difference if we all act together.

  e   Our world will be cleaner and healthier if we all use less and recycle more.

Practice

2   Make a mind map of key words and ideas from the sentences in Activity 1.

Challenge

3   Use the key words and ideas from Activity 2 to write a paragraph about recycling in
    your own words.

_____

_____

_____

_____

_____

〉 8.11 and 8.12 Create a magazine article

Language focus

Every text is different according to who it is for (audience), what it aims to
achieve (purpose), how it sounds (language) and how it looks (layout).

Focus

1   What magazines do you read?

_____

_____

_____

List five things you enjoy about reading a magazine.

_____

_____

_____

_____

_____

Practice

2   Choose and analyse a magazine article. Write the title and describe the magazine's audience, purpose, language and layout to complete the table.

Title: _____

Audience	Purpose	Language	Layout

Challenge

3   Research another environmental topic – 'The Great Pacific Garbage Patch'. Make notes using this mind map.

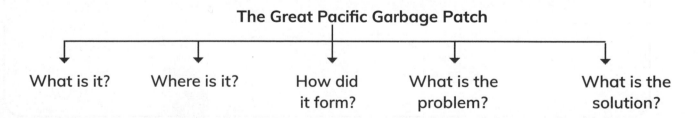

The Great Pacific Garbage Patch

What is it?   Where is it?   How did it form?   What is the problem?   What is the solution?

4 Plan a magazine article about 'The Great Pacific Garbage Patch'. Consider the audience, purpose, language and layout of your article. Write a first draft and edit it in the space provided. Then write it out neatly to display in class.

9 A moment in time

> 9.1 When you look at a painting

Focus

1   Reading poetry from around the word encourages us to find out more
about those countries. 'When You Look at a Painting' in the Learner's Book
Session 9.1 is by Guyanese poet Grace Nichols. Her country, Guyana, is
considered part of the Caribbean where they have many exotic fruits. Find
all the exotic fruits listed in the box in the wordsearch on the next page.
They may be written horizontally or diagonally!

banana	berries	breadfruit	cantaloupe	cherimoya	coconut
durian	granadilla	grapefruit	guava	jabuticaba	jackfruit
kiwi	kumquat	lychee	mangosteen	marula	mulberry
pawpaw	pineapple	pomegranate	rambutan	sapodilla	

A	K	J	C	A	K	M	U	E	I	O	C	B	P	N
Y	U	U	A	N	L	X	U	W	E	O	P	O	N	E
O	M	A	N	A	L	L	I	L	C	H	M	I	W	E
M	Q	S	T	I	F	K	I	O	B	E	C	J	M	T
I	U	A	A	R	D	A	N	D	G	E	A	Y	A	S
R	A	B	L	U	V	U	V	R	A	C	R	T	L	O
E	T	E	O	D	T	J	A	A	K	N	I	R	D	G
H	K	R	U	V	B	N	L	F	U	U	A	K	Y	N
C	T	R	P	M	A	L	R	F	R	G	X	R	W	A
Q	J	I	E	T	I	U	R	F	E	P	A	R	G	M
R	B	E	E	D	I	V	D	A	N	A	N	A	B	C
V	R	S	O	T	J	A	B	U	T	I	C	A	B	A
E	L	P	P	A	E	N	I	P	M	A	R	U	L	A
B	A	K	I	R	A	M	B	U	T	A	N	H	B	B
S	L	S	B	W	A	P	W	A	P	R	T	E	O	K

Practice

2 Research some of the fruits in Activity 1 and describe them.
Find out what country they are from.

Fruit	Description of the fruit	Where it's found

3   Choose a fruit that you enjoy. Describe this fruit literally (using adjectives and verbs) and then figuratively (using images).

A literal description of how the fruit looks, smells, feels and tastes

_____

_____

_____

_____

A figurative expression of the things it reminds you of, e.g. it is like … or it is a …

_____

_____

_____

_____

Fun images of what it might be doing, e.g. dressing up or blushing

_____

_____

_____

_____

Challenge

4 List a few tips that will help someone read a poem. Mention things they should notice and look out for when reading to help them to enjoy the poem and understand its deeper meaning.

Example: Look up difficult words and understand them in context.

Reading poetry is different from reading a story or a book. Poems have their own style. Each poem has its own special feeling and meaning.

How to read a poem for meaning

_____

_____

_____

_____

_____

_____

> 9.2 Poetic form and features

Focus

Poems come in many forms. Some poems have a set form while other poems have no form at all.

1   Match the types of poems to the features.
    You can join more than one feature to each poem type.

You might need to do independent research to find out the special features of some of these poetic forms.

Types of poems	Features
haiku	stanza
shape	rhythm
limerick	rhyme
couplet	no form
cinquain	shape
free verse	repetition
	set number of lines
	syllabification

Practice

2 Which types of poems do you enjoy? Give examples. Why do you enjoy them?

_____

_____

_____

_____

_____

_____

Challenge

3 Write your own definition for each of the following poetic devices used in poems:

a simile _____

b metaphor _____

c personification _____

d alliteration _____

e onomatopoeia _____

f assonance _____

> 9.3 There for a moment

Focus

Facts are useful to a writer, but a poem full of facts and nothing else would probably not make a creative or interesting poem. However, finding facts can help you write creatively.

1   Find a picture or draw an animal that appeals to you and write a catchy headline. The picture should be a snapshot of the animal, capturing a special moment, for example, a whale surfacing.

Maybe you could use a photograph of an animal that you took on holiday.

Practice

2   Carry out independent research to find ten facts about your chosen animal.

Example: Humpback whales are very acrobatic and can twirl around while surfacing.

_____

_____

_____

_____

_____

_____

_____

_____

_____

_____

Challenge

3   Choose six facts to write something descriptive or figurative about the animal.

Example: A surfacing whale is an acrobat twirling in the air. (metaphor)

_____

_____

_____

_____

_____

_____

> 9.4 Features for effect

Focus

How do you begin to write a poem? A good place to start is by knowing the answers to some important questions.

Use these key words to formulate your questions: pronouns, narrative voice, literal or figurative, poetic devices, style, mood, punctuation, line length.

1   Write out five questions that will help you to plan your own poem.

Example: What tense is the poem in?

Question 1 _____

Question 2 _____

Question 3 _____

Question 4 _____

Question 5 _____

Practice

2 Write five poetic features or effects you plan to use in your poem.

a _____

b _____

c _____

d _____

e _____

Challenge

3 Write a short poem demonstrating some of the features you listed above.

_____

_____

_____

_____

_____

_____

_____

_____

> 9.5 A jewel

Focus

Read an extract of the poem *How to Cut a Pomegranate.*

Just slit the upper skin across four quarters.
This is a magic fruit,
so when you split it open, be prepared
for the jewels of the world to tumble out,
more precious than garnets,
more lustrous than rubies,
lit as if from inside.

Imtiaz Dharker

1   Use your questions from Session 9.4 Activity 1 to analyse this extract of the poem.

   Example: What tense is it in? It is written in the present tense.

   a _____

   b _____

   c _____

   d _____

   e _____

Practice

2 Make up your own phrases using these words from the poem.

a More _____ than _____

b More _____ than _____

c More _____ than _____

d More _____ than _____

e More _____ than _____

Challenge

3 Write a short paragraph analysing the features of the poem extract.
Include the following terms.

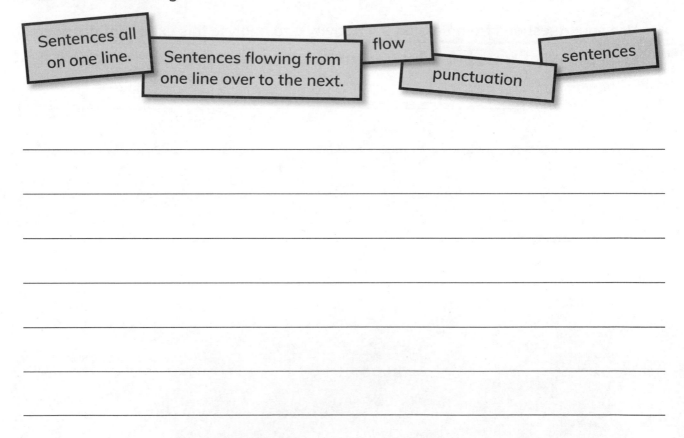

_____

_____

_____

_____

_____

_____

> 9.6 'Encapsulate' a moment in time

Focus

Narrative poetry tells a story. Use the animal facts you researched in Session 9.3 and your imagination to describe the 'story' of your animal.

1   Plan the poem using a mind map to capture ideas for images to encapsulate.

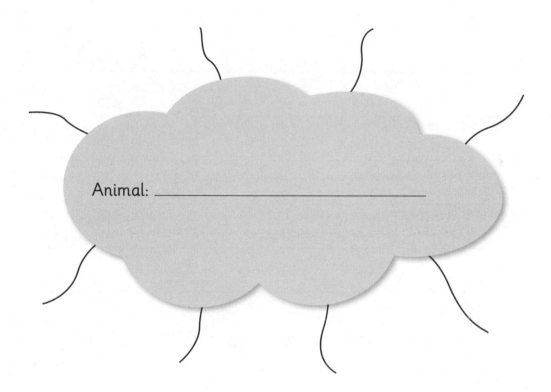

Animal: _____

Practice

2   Begin writing a first draft of your poem with the first lines of the poem *Impala*.

> Imagine, for a moment,
> As you lift your eyes
>
>   *Ted Townsend*

Title: _____

Imagine, for a moment,
As you lift your eyes

_____

_____

_____

_____

_____

_____

_____

_____

by _____

Challenge

3 Edit and improve your poem.

- Make sure it includes sentences that finish at the end of the line and sentences that flow from one line over into the next.

- Underline words that you can find more interesting synonyms for.

- Review your images to see if you can make them more vivid.

- Check your spelling and read your poem for flow and sense.

Then write out your final version neatly and illustrate it.

Title: _____

Imagine, for a moment,
As you lift your eyes

_____

_____

_____

_____

_____

_____

_____

_____

_____

by _____